The Truth in Tradition

THE TRUTH IN TRADITION

A Free Church Symposium

Keith W. Clements
Rupert E. Davies
David M. Thompson

edited by
Rupert E. Davies

EPWORTH PRESS

ISBN 0 7162 0479 7

First published 1992
by Epworth Press
1 Central Buildings
Westminster
London SW1H 9NR

Typeset by Intype Ltd, London
Printed in Great Britain by
Mackays of Chatham, Kent

Contents

Introduction

Everyone knows that there has been a vast change recently in the relations between the Christian churches. But one aspect of that change has frequently escaped notice.

For four centuries after the Reformation one of the chief bones of contention between Catholics and Protestants (and of some Protestants among themselves) was the interpretation of scripture. Each party in each dispute, adherents of Rome and Canterbury, Lutherans and Calvinists and Baptists, claimed to believe in the supreme authority of scripture. But when it came to their version of what scripture actually taught, and how it applied to the age in which they lived, they fell into disputation, erected impassable barriers against those who had different views, and even resorted to war.

The focus of these controversies was most frequently the Epistle to the Romans. Reading the commentaries on that book by Lutheran and Tridentine scholars leaves doubt in the mind as to whether they are dealing with the same book. But there are also innumerable passages elsewhere in the Bible of which the same is true.

This is no longer the case. The ecumenical study of the Bible, pursued by disinterested scholars who have controlled any desire to further the cause of their own denomination, has revealed many flaws in both the Catholic and the various Protestant interpretations so far offered. They have come to follow similar methods of exegesis, accepted common translations (as in the case of the Revised English Bible), and achieved a large agreement on the meaning of many books and passages which were previously areas of sharp dissension. Differences of emphasis and some matters of controversy still, of course, remain, but it is now perfectly possible for Catholics and Protestants to sit together round the same table and discuss the Epistle to the Romans in a spirit of goodwill and mutual helpfulness.

Attention has now shifted to another issue between and within the churches – an issue which has been lurking in the background since the dawn of ecumenism, and has emerged into prominence in recent years. It is the issue of tradition. This issue is most conspicuously alive at the moment within the Anglican communion in its dispute concerning the ordination of women to the priesthood. But it is also under constant discussion in all the inter-confessional conversations taking place in the present phase of ecumenical development.

Tradition, in the proper sense, may be defined as the body of teaching and liturgy which has been handed down, formulated and developed under the guidance of the Holy Spirit from the early ages of the church until the present day. (The definition in itself raises problems which will be handled later, but the general sense is perhaps clear.)

Tradition is certainly important in the life of every Christian communion, whether its importance is clearly stated or simply assumed. Probably the Orthodox Churches of the East set greater store by it than any other communion. But the Roman Catholic, Anglican and Protestant Churches are not very far behind.

Yet when we come to ask where tradition is to be found, and what its content is, differences of doctrine immediately appear, and it is these, or some of them, that form the subject of this book. The authors write from the standpoint of the English Free Churches, and they are moved to write in part because they cannot approve the doctrine of tradition which has gained the greatest degree of publicity in England, which is especially adduced by those who oppose women's ordination, and which sometimes seems to hold the field in ecumenical discussions.

Put in the directest terms, the doctrine consists in the assertion that tradition is faithfully preserved only in those communions which possess, as they claim, the historic succession of bishops from the apostles; that is, the Roman Catholic, Anglican and Orthodox communions. According to this view, what is officially taught and practised in these communions is genuine tradition; what is not so taught and practised, and especially anything at variance with what *is* taught and practised there, is not entitled to the name of tradition.

This doctrine is sometimes held in the strictest possible form, with the result that only the writings of the early Christian Fathers, the creeds of the undivided church, and certain historic liturgies are included in tradition. Usually it is held less stringently, and it is often conceded that some parts of tradition have spilled over into non-episcopal churches and validate some of their beliefs and practices, even allowing them a claim to sound theology. But in either case the holders of the doctrine are convinced that if anyone wishes to be sure of finding authentic and reliable tradition, it is to the episcopal churches that he or she must go.

It should, however, be added that within this doctrine there are two main ways of expounding tradition, and they are set out in the Final Report of the Anglican-Roman Catholic International Commission (ARCIC):

Tradition has been viewed in different ways. One approach is primarily concerned never to go beyond the bounds of Scripture. Under the guidance of the Spirit undiscovered values and truths are sought in the Scriptures to illuminate the faith according to the needs of each generation. This is not slavery to the text of Scripture. It is an unfolding of the riches of the original revelation. Another approach, while different, does not necessarily contradict the former. In the conviction that the Holy Spirit is seeking to guide the Church into the fullness of truth, it draws upon everything in human experience and thought which will give to the content of revelation its fullest expression and widest application. It is primarily concerned with the growth of the seed of God's word from age to age.[1]

All this, of course, within the episcopal churches.

The whole doctrine is unacceptable (not only to Free Church-people, but also to many Anglicans) for more than one reason. In the first place, when we ask on whose authority the limitation of tradition to the episcopal churches is affirmed we find that it is on the authority – not surprisingly – of the episcopal churches themselves. These churches have, in fact, set themselves up as judges in their own case. To put it otherwise, tradition is limited in a certain way on the ground of tradition, a perilously circular argument.

It may be replied to this that if we ask on whose authority the limitation of tradition is *denied*, the answer is – not surprisingly – that it is on the authority of the non-episcopal churches.

It is therefore perhaps more to the point to say that the 'limitation' view is in grave danger of reducing Christian faith and life to a narrow and rigid system, and it has frequently done so. Since the Reformation there have been innumerable men and women of God, prophets and teachers, who have been granted spiritual perceptions outside the bounds of any episcopal church. Such people have inspired and maintained whole Christian communities, and left an indelible mark on the history of the whole church of God. To deny these perceptions, *a priori*, a place in authentic Christian tradition is wholly inconsistent with the width and depth of God's wisdom and love, and, in the particular case of women's ordination, it deprives whole world-wide Christian communions of the fullness of the priesthood.

It has to be acknowledged, however, that the non-episcopal churches have done little in the way of expounding their own views of tradition. Indeed, for whatever reason, their silence

Introduction

has been so deafening as to arouse the suspicion that they have no respect for tradition and no teaching about it. The authors of this book try to begin to put this right. Each of them sets out the historical and present position of his own and kindred communions, and indicates, directly or indirectly, his personal approach to the matter. In this way it is hoped that the book will make a useful contribution to the current ecumenical discussions; and to numerous other debates in the churches now taking place.

Rupert E. Davies

A BAPTIST VIEW

Keith W. Clements

A chapter on Baptists and tradition might be expected to be very short. Baptists stand firmly within the stream of the Reformation and its principle of *sola scriptura*: no tradition subsequent to scripture, no teaching authority of the church, no creeds or councils, can vie with scripture as the authoritative seat of the saving knowledge of Jesus Christ and of the counsels of God by which the church is to be ordered and Christians are to conduct themselves. But Baptists claim to have ventured further into this stream than most. Their rejection of infant baptism in favour of believers' baptism is based on their reading of the New Testament. In rejecting infant baptism they reject one of the most venerable and universal traditions of Christianity, and thereby they invest even more in the authority of scripture, as against tradition, than do others of the Protestant and Free Church family. The Separatists of the late sixteenth and early seventeenth centuries, out of whom English Baptists arose, had already made scripture the touchstone of church order. The question of true baptism, following upon that of true membership, led certain of them to a re-examination of the scriptures and – one might almost say incidentally or at least unexpectedly – to a new understanding of the relationships between water-baptism and personal confession of faith. Having once occupied *that* position, at odds with the rest of doctrinally orthodox Christianity, the Baptists were inevitably committed

6

to an even more stalwart defence of the route – scriptural authority – which had led them there.

This attitude to scripture over against tradition is of course determinative of much more than baptismal theology and practice, notably, for example, the congregational or gathered-church principle. But it is important to note that in Baptist thought scriptural authority has meant not so much the authority of 'the book' *per se*, as the authority of the living word of God speaking through it. The supreme authority is Jesus Christ himself, as made known through inspired study of the inspired scripture. For Baptists as for Luther 'by scripture alone' means 'by Christ alone'. Or, as the first clause in the Baptist Union Declaration of Principle puts it: 'That our Lord Jesus Christ, God manifest in the flesh, is the sole and absolute authority in all matters pertaining to faith and practice, *as revealed in the Holy Scriptures*, and that each church has liberty under the guidance of the Holy Spirit, to interpret and administer His Laws' (emphases mine).

Baptists therefore claim to find Christ more assuredly in the scriptures, not tradition. Typical is a statement in the reply of the Baptist Union Assembly of 1926 to the 'Appeal to All Christian People' issued by the 1920 Lambeth Conference: 'The Scriptures, in and through which the Spirit of God speaks possess for us supreme and unique authority. While we recognize the historic value of ancient creeds, we cannot give them a place of authority comparable to that of the Scriptures.'[1] E. A. Payne, one of the most authoritative British Baptist voices this century, well described his denomination's ethos: 'They have claimed the guidance of the living Spirit of Jesus Christ present within his church, a guidance inspired, confirmed and held in check by appeal to the Scriptures and, in particular, to those of the New Testament. The final court of appeal has been neither to church pronouncements, nor to history and tradition as such, but to the conscience of the church inspired by the Spirit of God as a result of the study of the Bible.'[2]

The reserved attitude of Baptists to tradition in relation to scripture quickly becomes clear. But equally, a careful reading of even the few statements cited thus far should indicate why this chapter cannot in fact be brief. Scripture is exalted to a unique position of authority above tradition: but tradition is not thereby damned out of existence. Implicitly, it has some significance for the understanding of Christian truth and life; the question is just *what* significance.

We shall return presently to this general question. For the moment it is worth noting that the word 'tradition' itself does in fact belong firmly within the Baptist vocabulary, if not so much in the larger sense then at least with certain particular and positive usages. Baptists have now been in existence for nearly four centuries, more than long enough to have acquired a distinctive history to own and cherish (the 'heritage'), an identity shaped by struggle and circumstance over the generations. In short, a tradition, and one which moreover is virtually as old as the Anglican settlement. Indeed at various times in Baptist history there has appeared one form or another of the doctrine of 'successionism', the theory of a continuity of 'Baptist' practice from New Testament times onwards and throughout Christian history, sometimes hidden from view in subterranean movements, at other times surfacing in radical minority groups until the appearance of the radical, anabaptist wing of the Reformation and English Separatism. Such a theory has not been felt to be worth the attention of serious scholars for quite some time now, and indeed it serves polemical rather than genuinely historical interests, polemical interests which in fact are strangely at odds with a primal loyalty to scripture. Well did an eighteenth-century American Baptist historian state:

Uninterrupted succession is a specious lure, a snare set by

sophistry, into which all parties have fallen: and it hath happened to spiritual genealogists as it hath to others who have traced natural descents: both have wattled together twigs of any kind to fill up remote chasms. The doctrine is necessary only to such churches as regulate their faith and practice by tradition, and for their use it was first invented.[3]

A sense of the tradition connecting the undoubted seventeenth-century Baptist origins with the present is another matter. This kind of sense is of course shared with the other Free Churches, but it was the Baptist E. A. Payne who powerfully undergirded this awareness with his significantly titled book, *The Free Church Tradition in the Life of England*, published in 1944.[4] The date as well as the title was significant, for towards the end of the Second World War British people were alert with the expectation of a new order for their post-war lives, of values they had desperately fought the war to preserve yet which had now to be fully incarnated in a more just, free and equal society. Payne was articulating the claim that the Free Church 'tradition' involving freedom of conscience before God, the priesthood of all believers and the separation of church from state, had been central to the long-running creative forces in British social history and now needed developing for the new ecumenical and political era.

In this sense Baptists – and no doubt other Free Church people could say the same for themselves – have been no less 'tradition-conscious' as Anglicans and Roman Catholics in this country, at least when their distinctive claims and identity have been at issue. In the last decade the identity-question has become crucial for those Baptists, in Britain and elsewhere, most affected by the charismatic movement. Traditionally (the word slips out automatically!) Baptist church order is that of the gathered fellowship of believers who corporately seek the mind of Christ in their decision-making through the 'church meeting', in which all members partake. Certain forms of charismatic evangelicalism have been pressing the case for a more authoritarian form of church leadership in which pastor and 'elders' exercise a more directive role over the membership, in some cases to the point of prescribing what the Spirit is saying to the church there and then. Is a church governed by such means truly 'Baptist'? The answers involve what one thinks is the authentic Baptist 'tradition' running from the seventeenth century to the present or, alternatively, what one thinks of that tradition anyhow and whether one considers that the ultimate Baptist trait of scriptural authority now demands a yet more far-reaching reformation of 'traditional' Baptist patterns of church life and ministry to accord with the New Testament.[5]

This kind of historic tradition is not, admittedly, what is meant by 'tradition' in the larger sense of an authoritative corpus of teachings and practices, additional to scripture, by which Christian truth has been 'handed on' from apostolic times to the present. That it exists, however, has an important bearing on the attitude of Baptists to 'tradition' in this larger sense. That attitude, we have noted, vigorously asserts the supreme authority of scripture over all other claimants, including tradition. 'The whole counsel of God,' states the Second London Confession of 1677 and 1688, 'concerning all things necessary for his own glory, man's salvation, faith and life, is either expressly set down or necessarily contained in the holy scripture; unto which nothing at any time is to be added, whether by new revelation of the Spirit, or traditions of men.'[6] Such a conviction cannot accept the classic Roman Catholic position set out at the Council of Trent which states of revelation that 'this truth and this discipline are contained in written books and in unwritten tradition'. Nor does it sit easily with Article XXXIV of the Church of England, which temperately enjoins recognition of those 'traditions and ceremonies of the Church, which be not repugnant to the Word of God, and be ordained and approved by common authority': tradition in the words of a modern

Anglican writer, 'as a necessary part of the Christian faith, but tradition judged by and found agreeable to scripture'.[7]

Such statements, to the Baptist mind, affirm tradition while conceding the final say to scripture, whereas Baptists would prefer to affirm scripture while conceding a subsidiary place to tradition. The subsidiary place of tradition is none the less real. For example, while Baptists are typically conscious of what they have felt to be various misuses of credal formulae, they have never disowned the great historic creeds of the ancient church. At the inauguration of the Baptist World Alliance in London in 1905, the first meeting opened with the solemn recitation of the Apostles' Creed by all present, as a signal testimony that the gathering felt itself to belong to the one great family of catholic and apostolic Christianity. This was by no means wholly alien to the Baptist tradition. The 'Orthodox Creed' produced by the General (i.e. Arminian) Baptists of 1678, having asserted the holy scripture to be the divinely authoritative source 'of all things necessary for salvation', and that 'no decrees of popes, or councils, or writings of any person whatsoever, are of equal authority with the holy scriptures' proceeds to urge that the Nicene, Athanasian and Apostles' Creeds 'ought thoroughly to be received and believed'.[8] Such creeds, according to the Baptist authors, are validated by scripture and of great utility in summarily teaching the biblical faith and in refuting heresy.

Baptists in the second half of the twentieth century have by and large held consistently to the supremacy of scripture as the authoritative source of revelation. This has not necessarily implied a 'conservative' attitude to biblical study, still less a fundamentalism. All along, we have noted, Baptists have believed that scripture is authoritative because therein is heard the authoritative voice of the living and sovereign Christ. Such an understanding is quite capable of accommodating historical and critical study of the documents, indeed, some would say, demanding such tools for greater understanding. From about the mid-century onwards Baptist scholarship and theological education, like that of other denominations in Britain, caught some of the influence of the neo-orthodoxy of Karl Barth and Emil Brunner (perhaps especially the latter): the word of God is the word made flesh, Jesus Christ himself, encountered in the word proclaimed, attested by the word written. The Bible can be seen and studied thoroughly as a 'human' set of documents – yes, even as a collection of human 'tradition'. But this does not detract from the transcendent reality to which it bears witness, the gospel. Indeed, that gospel itself historically precedes scripture, and has its own 'handing on', the *paradosis*, first oral, then written. In Baptist understanding, it is the transmission of that apostolic gospel which constitutes acceptable 'tradition'. A contemporary Baptist, Neville Clark, has written

> There can be no question of apostolic succession as *usually* understood. The Church lives by the word of God once for all spoken in Jesus Christ and made known to her, in the time between ascension and parousia, through the controlling witness of the apostles. Inexorably and inescapably we are driven back to the historical Jesus as we seek encounter with the risen Lord. It is for this reason that the holy scriptures must perpetually remain normative for the Church's life. They are the abiding deposit of apostolic testimony, the earthly vehicle of historical revelation; and by her subjection to them the Church manifests her faithful obedience to her ruling head. It is by reference to scripture and in dependence upon scripture that the body of Christ, ordered by the apostolic Gospel, proclaims the apostolic kerygma; and in that proclamation the living word moves forth anew to gather in the elect and the people of God move outward to the ends of the earth and forward to the end of time.[9]

This in outline states the Baptist perspective on tradition: a matter for rigorous scrutiny in the light of the normative, apostolic testimony to be found in scripture. It is an overtly critical perspective, well illustrated for example by a statement in the response of the Baptist Union of Great Britain to the recent Faith and Order 'Lima' text *Baptism, Eucharist and Ministry*, where each responding church is asked, among other matters, to indicate 'the extent to which your church can recognize in this text the faith of the church through the ages.'[10] The Baptist response confesses difficulty with the question itself:

> We do not find this form of question particularly meaningful or significant. We can recognize in this text a multitude of emphases in harmony with the witness of the New Testament, and in our response we have thankfully acknowledged key areas where this is judged to be so. *But tradition is a dynamic process with inevitable admixture of truth and error*; and formulations of faith change through the ages, not least because of changing contexts and situations. What we register is a valuable contemporary movement towards common understanding on divisive issues (emphases mine).[11]

A critical slant, however, is not the same as an inherently dismissive or negative attitude. On the contrary, it is just because tradition has such a proper importance of its own that it has to be subjected to such critical examination. (One might, by analogy, say that the reason why Baptists can be such stern sermon-critics is precisely because of the importance they attach to preaching, the human handing-on or *paradosis* of the word of God, each sermon being effectively a moment of tradition in action). I do not wish to argue the Baptist case for this any further. Rather, having delineated the Baptist approach, it would be a more creative exercise now to set it in the context of the wider debate about 'tradition' so that we might begin to assess what its present and future ecumenical significance might be.

In our time, the opposition between scripture and tradition has become blurred and softened, if not actually dissolved, by a number of factors. Not least in importance here has been historical and critical study of the apostolic and post-apostolic periods of the early church. Where does scripture end and tradition begin? Why should II Peter be canonical but the *Didache* not so? And if the formation of the canon was not completed until well towards the end of the second century, is it not likely that the unwritten tradition, the *rule of faith* so important to Irenaeus and others, was vital in determining that canon of scripture? Is not talk of 'scripture or tradition' a putting asunder of what history has joined together?

In addition, however, certain ecclesiastical and ecumenical statements during the past thirty years or so have sought to overcome the polarities of the 'scripture versus tradition' mindset inherited from the controversies of the sixteenth century and later. Or perhaps more accurately, some of these statements have been *read* as seeking to overcome these polarities. Indeed, as long ago as 1968, the Scottish theologian Ronald Gregor Smith, in one of the finest pieces of writing on the subject,[12] complained of a rather confusing tendency of Protestant and Catholic theologians almost to swop positions on this matter. Here I will only mention two relevant documents: one from the Second Vatican Council, the other from the Fourth World Conference on Faith and Order in Montreal, 1963.

The statement from Vatican II, the *Dogmatic Constitution on Divine Revelation*, was issue on November 18 1965. Few documents from the Council have had more ecumenical influence, or at any rate have provoked more interest and discussion, than this. It speaks of revelation as being not primarily the issuing of doctrinal propositions from above, but God's saving impartation of his own self, in deeds and words, the sharing of himself and his own life for the salvation of humankind, the innermost truth of this revelation shining forth in Christ, 'who is himself both the mediator and the sum total of revelation'.[13] Although it keeps a place for natural theology, much of this resonates with the tones of modern Protestant theology as struck by such as Karl Barth. Chapter II of the document, 'The Transmission of Divine Revelation', describes how the revelation set out in the gospel was, under the command of Christ, faithfully handed on by the apostles in their teaching, in their exemplary lives, in the institutions they established, and in their writing: 'it was done by those apostles and other men associated with the apostles who, under the inspiration of the same Holy Spirit, committed the message of salvation to writing'.[14] 'This sacred Tradition, then, and the sacred Scripture of both Testaments, are like a mirror, in which the Church, during her pilgrim journey here on earth, contemplates God, from whom she receives everything, until such time as she is brought to see him face to face as he really is'.[15] Thus it is the apostolic preaching of the gospel, expressed in a special way in the inspired books, which is to be preserved through the teaching succession within the church to the end of time, with the help of the Holy Spirit. There is not only preservation but growth in insight into the truth. 'Thus, as the centuries go by, the Church is always advancing towards the plentitude of divine truth, until eventually the words of God are fulfilled in her.'[16] Through this dynamic, Spirit-led process of tradition in which God converses with his people, the scriptures themselves 'are more thoroughly understood and actualized in the Church'.[17] Paragraphs 9 and 10 deserve quoting almost in full:

9. Sacred Tradition and sacred Scripture, then, are bound

15

closely together, and communicate one with the other. For both of them, flowing out from the same divine well-spring, come together in some fashion to form one thing, and move towards the same goal. Sacred Scripture is the speech of God as it is put down in writing under the breath of the Holy Spirit. And Tradition transmits in its entirety the Word of God which has been entrusted to the apostles by Christ the Lord and the Holy Spirit . . . Thus it comes about that the Church does not draw her certainty about all revealed truths from the holy Scriptures alone. Hence, both Scripture and Tradition must be accepted and honored with equal feelings of devotion and reverence.

10. Sacred Tradition and sacred Scripture make up a single sacred deposit of the Word of God, which is entrusted to the Church. By adhering to it the entire holy people, united to its pastors, remains always faithful to the teaching of the apostles, to the brotherhood, to the breaking of bread and the prayers (cf. Acts 2.42).

The statement, having taken this 'both and' line in relation to scripture and tradition, proceeds in what many have considered to be a highly ambiguous paragraph to reaffirm the 'living teaching office of the Church alone' as providing the authentic interpretation of the Word of God, while also saying that 'this Magisterium is not superior to the Word of God, but its servant'.[18] Sacred tradition, sacred scripture and the magisterium of the church form an interdependent whole. Perhaps what non-Catholics found so heartening in the whole document, however, was the extensive treatment given in the remaining chapters to scripture – its inspiration, its study and its place in the life of the church. If tradition and the magisterium were also emphasized, then at least they were not superior to or independent of scripture.

Two years earlier, in 1963, the Fourth World Conference on

Faith and Order at Montreal had produced a report on Scripture, Tradition and Traditions. In this document lie certain paragraphs which in recent years have been quoted with increasing frequency in Faith and Order circles on account of their unitive possibilities. Thus:

> Our starting-point is that we are all living in a tradition which goes back to our Lord and has its roots in the Old Testament, and are all indebted to that tradition inasmuch as we have received the revealed truth, the Gospel, through its being transmitted from one generation to another. Thus we can say that we exist as Christians by the Tradition of the Gospel . . . testified in Scripture, transmitted in and by the Church through the power of the Holy Spirit. Tradition taken in this sense is actualized in the preaching of the Word, in the administration of the Sacraments and worship, in Christian teaching and theology, and in mission and witness to Christ by the lives of the members of the Church.
>
> What is transmitted in the process of tradition is the Christian faith, not only as a sum of tenets, but as a living reality transmitted through the operation of the Holy Spirit.[19]

The document now becomes more subtle, at least in its English version. Thus:

> We can speak of the Christian Tradition (with a capital T), whose content is God's revelation and self-giving in Christ, present in the life of the Church.
>
> But this Tradition which is the work of the Holy Spirit is embodied in traditions (in the two senses of the word, both as referring to diversity in forms of expression, and in the sense of separate communions). The traditions in

Christian history are distinct from, and yet connected with, the Tradition. They are the expressions and manifestations in diverse historical forms of the one truth and reality which is Christ.[20]

Vatican II and Montreal have exemplified and encouraged an eirenic manner of speaking about the transmission of revelation: it is the apostolic teaching, or the gospel, which is the core of revelation, which has come into history and which is transmitted through the Christian centuries under the guidance of the Spirit. Vatican II speaks of 'a single, sacred deposit', Montreal of Tradition with a capital T. Such statements express a holistic approach, encompassing both scripture and its subsequent interpretation, which is typically summed up inclusively as 'tradition'. So what we often find now is reference to 'the Christian tradition' as that main thrust of Christian belief through time to the present. Some of us have come to use such phraseology almost as a matter of course, not least in discussion of ethical issues. We want to bring 'the insights of the Christian tradition' – the 'Christian tradition' of the just war, or the sanctity of life, or the primacy of love or whatever – to bear on contemporary debates. One suspects that at times what is being sought is some amiable middle term which will avoid the embarrassments of either 'biblical authority' or 'magisterial authority', some expression of the thought of 'the church of the ages' from scripture onwards which will be self-authenticating to all Christian minds seeking consensus. A contemporary Anglican, Paul Avis, in his critical review of the ARCIC proposals, argues that the idea of the *consensus fidelium* has proved attractive to Anglicans wanting a way round the intractable problems of papal authority and infallibility, and equally attractive to those Catholics wanting to present to their partners in dialogue 'the acceptable face of Catholicism'. 'As a result "the mind of the Church" has become one of the most overworked concepts of modern ecclesiology.'[21]

Speaking of 'the Christian tradition' or 'the mind of the church' may be a useful shorthand. It could, however, be a misleading attempt at a short cut. A closer examination of Vatican II and Montreal shows that some basic questions are left open and some are not even asked. We may notice in the Vatican II statement a surprisingly loose wording which speaks of scripture and tradition 'coming together *in some fashion* to form one thing, and move toward the same goal' (emphases mine). What fashion?, we may well ask. The whole question of how in fact we appropriate the tradition, of how we retrieve the past in any sense and enable it to become present, is not raised, although it has been a matter of keen debate since early in the nineteenth century in Protestantism, and more recently in Catholicism (see for example the work of Karl Rahner). It is the whole question of how we come to an understanding of writings from the past, the problem of hermeneutics. What is made clear however in Vatican II is the continuing and crucial role of the church's teaching office, the magisterium. Montreal, for its part, is certainly quite frank about the inherent problems in its formulation; the trouble is that those eirenic paragraphs quoted earlier are habitually cited out of context. The Montreal document in fact goes on to admit that there are difficulties in establishing the criteria for Tradition (capital T), that there are profound disagreements on what the criteria should be. We can talk about 'interpretation' of scripture in the 'Tradition', but what is right interpretation? But there is an even more fundamental difficulty which the report scarcely recognizes, namely, what exactly is meant by 'Tradition' (capital T) anyway? It is certainly something that one would wish to exist, an objective source of unimpeachable truth, of pure belief unaffected by time and chance, beyond the vagaries and prejudices of our particular confessional and partisan standpoints. But is there, can there be, anything beyond these particular visible traditions? Once traditions in their plurality are acknowledged, any notion of a single great 'Tradition' over and above these becomes a dubious Will o' the Wisp. We are tempted to suspect that what may be going on here is that old theological game of let's pretend, of imagining that because a word is used, especially a word with a capital letter, what it refers to has a real existence.

These might seem to be cavilling objections based on mere theory and semantics, when at the very least a way has been opened up for Christians of diverse confessional standpoints to feel at home with 'tradition' as a continuing process of encounter with the word of God, a kind of sum total of all the truth into which the Spirit leads. But even if there did exist such a tradition which we could identify, there would remain the question of whether it was something we could wholly identify *with*. In the last twenty years or so any straightforward appreciation of 'tradition' has met with some formidable objections of a quite immediate kind. Just when it seemed that it was quite safe for us to go into these waters and swim with the warm currents of the 'faith of the church of the ages', some sinister monsters have been found lurking in the depths of 'the tradition'. Two examples may be cited of sightings which, in the west at any rate, have prompted many to beat it quickly back towards the beach.

First, the enormity of the Jewish holocaust has demanded a fresh appraisal of the role of anti-semitism in Christian life and thought down the ages. Hitherto theologians and church leaders have felt able to dismiss the remarks of some of the church fathers, or of certain Popes, or of Luther, as accidental aberrations or excesses. Now the question is being put, as to whether anti-semitism is not much more central in the Christian tradition, in fact as deeply rooted as some of the doctrines which are consciously considered essential to Christian belief. Might anti-semitism even be, as Rosemary Radford Ruether has argued, the reverse side of a christology which makes absolutist claims for Jesus as Son of God and thereby implicitly rejects all Jewish understandings of Messiahship?[22] And what then happens if this anti-Jewish tradition is seen to be not just a later distortion of the scriptural witness, but traceable right back into the New Testament itself?

Second, there has been the critique by feminist theology of the patriarchal society, the patriarchal church and the patriarchal God. As with the exposure of Christian anti-semitism, no sanctuary has been permitted within some apparently 'authentic' Christian tradition as opposed to the 'distortions' of actual history. It is no use claiming that what the church has actually taught and done down the ages in promoting partiarchalism in society and religion was accidental to its 'real beliefs'.

In face of such critiques arising from contemporary experience and moral sensibility, to speak of 'the Christian tradition' in such a generalized sense and to regard it as authoritative is exceedingly problematical. In July 1989 a conference of British and South African theologians took place in Cambridge. At one session there was much discussion of how in both the British and South African contexts the role of theology is, in some such words, 'to bring the insights of the Christian tradition to bear on the social realities'. At length one of the South Africans, a white radical, rose to say that in South Africa it is in fact the 'Christian tradition' itself which is being brought to judgment by the social realities; that it is no use asking what insight might be drawn from, for example, Augustine, since Augstine's legacy might itself be part of the problem in South Africa today. In the last two decades of the twentieth century, theology does indeed seem to be taking a long farewell to innocence as far as its past is concerned.

We cannot completely cut loose from tradition without losing Christian identity. 'Without a firm and solid grip on the past out of which we have come, there can be no order, no clear line, and thus no future', states Ronald Gregor Smith.[23] To lose that identity is of course an option we could take out of commitment to contemporary human and religious concerns, if it was felt that the past has absolutely nothing more to offer us. But so long as we identify in any sense with Christianity, and so as long as Christianity lays any claim to stem from a revelation in history, we must somehow also be able to say that faith extends *through* history, *through* time, connecting us in our contemporary context with that which burst upon the scene once upon a time in Palestine. That means a tradition, a handing on from one time to another. Unless we believe in the repetition of purely mystical experiences, that tradition, even if ascribed to the continual inspiration of the Holy Spirit, must also be a very human affair of writing, reading and hearing. But if, humanly speaking, this is a very suspect affair, how can we identify with it in all the passion of faith? What are the terms on which a contemporary, critically aware faith might accept the role of tradition? What kind of authority can we accord it? And can we invest it with any kind of authority if we do not make some kind of distinction between it on the one hand, and the apostolic faith or gospel which it claims to transmit, on the other?

'Tradition' or 'the Christian tradition' can only be saved as a concept if too much is not made of it, that is, if it is distinguished from the apostolic faith as such and kept in its proper place relative to that original proclamation. That is the significance for ecumenical dialogue of a position such as the Baptist which insists on the absolute priority of the scriptures as normative for faith and life. Attempt to make 'tradition' in general the vehicle of Christian truth or the bearer of authority, and it collapses under its own weight – or we collapse under it – because of itself it lacks any criterion by which its authenticity may be judged. That implies not just a belief that there is an original 'apostolic faith', but a historical sense that we can know what in essentials it is.

To explore this issue a little further, a brief dialogue with a contemporary Anglican may be appropriate, albeit one who has been in controversy with some sections of his communion. In the writings of David Jenkins, Bishop of Durham, there is a lot about the doctrinal tradition, as may be seen in his sermons and papers *Living with Questions*, now up-dated as *Still Living with Questions*.[24] In his 1964 paper 'How much Doctrine do we Need?' he speaks of the threefold cord of tradition, experience and the policy of common living, as the means by which the truth of the gospel is assured to us. He calls for dynamic doctrine: 'we take the doctrines which the tradition which hands us the gospel has handed to us and we submit them to the questions which our speaking of the universe has raised for them, and we submit the current dogmas of our speaking of the universe to the questioning of the doctrines'.[25] He fears, rightly in my view, a *finality* of tradition, indeed a finality of theology. As he says powerfully in his 1965 sermon 'What is There to Know?': 'the only theology which does justice to the reality defined by Jesus Christ is a broken theology in which all theories are systematically and constantly being broken up so that they may be open to further possibilities'.[26] To which I would only add that if there is indeed a built-in obsolesence in all theology, this might actually mean that we have to handle with some care the legacies we have received from the past so as to get best use out of them for as long as possible, especially if for the present we don't know what will replace them.

In his recent book *God, Miracle and the Church of England*[27] in particular Part Two entitled 'Anglicanism, Accident and Providence', and above all in the chapter 'What is Church History?' Bishop Jenkins seeks an understanding of God as universally and graciously at work in 'interactive' rather than 'intervening' ways, and wants to bring this understanding to bear on how a church – and specifically the Church of England – conceives of its status and function today. Appeals to the past can no longer be made to substantiate absolutist claims. Historical reflection, we realize today, is a very subjective affair. Church history is largely 'made up' and 'propaganda' to suit particular contemporary interests. Anglicanism today, instead of justifying itself by illusory appeals to tradition, must, with other communions, view itself in the perspective of God's open, future-oriented activity concerned with the well-being of the entire human community. He argues persuasively for a dynamic and outward-looking ecumenism, and as a Free Church person I am greatly encouraged by the breadth and generosity of Bishop Jenkins' vision. I find, too, that certain of his criticisms of Anglican history-making can find parallel targets within my own 'tradition'. For instance, Ian Sellars has written a neat exposure of the shifting ways in which Baptist historians have regarded Baptist origins.[28] Especially problematic in our origins is the question of what historical continuity, if any, there was between the continental Anabaptist movements which began in the early days of the sixteenth-century Reformation and the first Baptist congregations of the early seventeenth century. Sellars goes a long way to showing that much American and British Baptist historiography since the mid-nineteenth century has by turns been enamoured of, or embarrassed by, the possibility of such links, and that these changes in historical opinion show a marked correlation with Baptist social and theological stances of the day. At times when Baptists have seen themselves as belonging to the mainstream of orthodoxy and upholders of established social attitudes, fit company to sup with bishops, their historians have tended to distance early Baptists from the dangerously radical wing of the Reformation represented by the Anabaptists. When Baptists have wished to identify with more radical social and religious movements of their own day, they have been more eager to discern some kind of blood-relationship with Anabaptism.

But Jenkins, I feel, leaves us with what seems like an incoherent understanding of history which will not in the end support the dynamism he wants. While rightly warning us against the selective and propagandist use of (church) history, he gives us little guidance on how we could recognize the *responsible use* of history – or if there is any such use at all. Thus 'all such church history is propaganda and bound to be', and 'history, as well as being interpreted, is being made up with a view to how history shall now go on'. Well and good; the irreducibly subjective element in historical study has been widely accepted ever since Wilhelm Dilthey recognized it in the last century, and has repeatedly been affirmed by thinkers as diverse as Martin Heidegger, R.G. Collingwood and Karl Rahner. But some of Jenkins' statements come close to being blanket dismissals of all historical reconstruction. That is a rather serious position for a Christian theologian to be in. For what, we may ask, is the relation between 'church history' (of which Bishop Jenkins is highly suspicious) and what is usually termed biblical history, or at least the story of Jesus? Are the 'stories about Jesus' any less 'made up' than much 'church history'? Bishop Jenkins, as a highly incarnational theologian, wants to say that the Jesus-stories are central for belief in God. But how do we know that the stories as we have them were any less made up by the early church to suit its own propaganda purposes than the later histories of the church were made up to suit certain ecclesiastical self-interests? Bishop Jenkins' interest in Jesus, who he was and what he did, all of which is the decisive disclosure of God to us, implies a heavy investment in history as such, which he does not seem willing to make. But does not a belief in the 'apostolic faith' require some such investment?

It is clear what Jenkins wished to avoid: a static fixity of tradition claiming absolute validity for all time, preventing faith from facing the challenges of service and witness in the world of today and tomorrow, a ball-and-chain mindlessly fettering the church to an illusory past. He wants an open, dynamic, future-oriented church. He wants it shaped according to the figure of Jesus as the incarnate revelation of God. But his seeming aversion to taking past history seriously would seem to be inconsistent with that Jesus-based faith. In an odd way, his position is that of an extremist advocate of scripture over against tradition, but without any rationale for holding scripture – and therefore Jesus – to be any more historically accessible than the later tradition which is behind a smokescreen of historical scepticism.

Can we be interested in historical reconstruction and tradition on the one hand, while on the other hand being open and dynamic in the way Bishop Jenkins wants?

I believe the answer is yes. In fact I would argue that a historical concern is a prerequisite for being dynamically open to the future, for only so can we be liberated from the shackles of what often masquerades as 'tradition', recovering what is more truly the 'tradition' and, still more importantly, the apostolic gospel at its source. (A sense of tradition of course is crucially important not only in the Christian community but in any human social enterprise. It is a dimension of our sociality, a sociality which extends through time. Our heritage is our power.) But this requires that we have a significant confidence in our ability to know the past. By a 'significant confidence' I do not mean a positivist claim to final knowledge of 'precisely what happened'. As I said earlier, we need to acknowledge an essential subjectivity in historiography. But historical accounts can claim validity in so far as they are open to testing and challenge by other accounts. At the very least we can be made aware of our subjectivities through encounter with others' perspectives.

But more important still, it is precisely that rootedness in the apostolic faith, that continual return to the history recorded in the bible, that drives us dynamically forward. This is what both creates tradition and moves it forward to new possibilities. Tradition is at least in part what we create out of our history. There is no given tradition which is authoritative simply because it is tradition, speaking authoritatively for itself and authenticating itself. Its authority is always derivative from the gospel of which it claims to be the vehicle. We are necessarily back with the polarity and indeed distinction between scripture and tradition, of tradition under the critical scrutiny of what is found in scripture, in place of the rather blandly holistic 'Christian tradition'. The primacy lies in scripture – but note, *in* scripture. The word of God is Jesus, to which all the human words about him point, including the words of scripture. To find the burning point of revelation we go not to tradition as such, but to the scriptures. And not quite to the scriptures as such, but to that to which the scriptures in all their humanness are witnesses, and within them we discern the light in the darkness. As a contemporary Baptist, Christopher Ellis, puts it, 'Even the church of the New Testament must be tested against its Lord before we can follow in its way.'[29] Between an authoritative word of God in scripture and an authoritative church there is no amiable 'middle way' to be found in the concept of 'tradition' as such.

But far from making tradition of no account, as earlier Protestantism tended to do, we could now be in a position to give it a proper basis. The trouble with earlier emphases upon tradition was the implication of finality, the definitively true interpretation of the archetypally true scripture: belief sanctified by time, or as it has been described, tradition as a heap from which nothing may be removed (though presumably things may be mysteriously added while no one is looking). So too there was an absolutism ascribed to scripture which seemed almost to make the Bible itself divine rather than the witness to the divine. The feminist theologian Elisabeth Schüssler Fiorenza argues that it is wrong to regard scripture as an archetype, an 'ideal form that establishes an unchanging timeless pattern',[30] and suggests instead that we think of it as a *prototype*, something critically open to its own transformation. A difficulty with this alternative image being applied to scripture is that we cannot actually transform scripture, still less can scripture transform itself, although our *understanding* of scripture and the way we read it may well change. But Fiorenza's suggestion has a sound touch on the biblical dynamic, the paradox that in looking back to the New Testament we are immediately directed *forwards* to the eschaton, the great fulfilment. Biblical faith is categorically futuristic. By contrast, so much of our discussion about belief is purely past-oriented, and it is assumed that our faithfulness to what was supposedly at the beginning is the sole measure of the validity of our belief and practice. Faithfulness to the gospel involves faithfulness not just to its past but to that future where will be realized completely the new humanity and the fullness of the presence of God. It is an experimental, enter-prising faith seeking ways of being signs of the divine end in Christ rather than forever returning to the chronological beginning.

It is striking that some elements in the tradition which are now regarded as venerable beyond question, were in their time seen as dangerous second-bests. The great example is of how almost accidentally *homoousion* – 'of one substance with' – came into the Nicene debate in the fourth century, and how diffidently it was regarded for a time even by those (traditionalists!) upholding the 'catholic' trinitarian theology. A non-scriptural term was found to be the best vehicle for the scriptural faith in the context of fourth-century Hellenistic culture. Tradition is the series of experiments in life and doctrine, worship and ethics, applications of the original scriptural prototype, on how we conceive and live the kingdom of God which in its fullness is still ahead of us and beyond us. There is a provisionality in all tradition. 'Provisional' should not be seen as a negative term; after all it means 'seeing before, fore-seeing'. Some experiments prove dud failures. Some last a very long time, are seasoned and matured in the experience of generations, and become the acquired wisdom for nurturing and guiding the people of God. But none can escape testing against the normative patterns of scripture, and without that examination the tradition itself eventually dies, either through obesity or undernourishment. 'The tradition . . . and in particular the doctrinal tradition, is truly itself only when it throws itself away. That is, it is not the last word, just as it is not the first word. It is only within the dynamism of history as the place and the time of irreversible personal decisions that the Word is truly heard, and faith is truly active.'[31]

It might be argued that the view of the relation between scripture and tradition which I have suggested could, for example, admit the ordination of women but also the baptism of infants. We do not read of women bishops or elders in the New Testament, but Baptists now ordain women ministers. Why then should Baptists object if other churches now baptize infants, a practice for which the New Testament evidence is admittedly slight? Why is the former a legitimate departure from scripture, the latter not so? Why is one a legitimate development in tradition, the latter invalid? The answer most Baptists would give would be, in effect: the calling of God to minister in leadership of the church, as that ministry is defined in the New Testament, is not theologically tied to gender. To be called to be a servant of the servant people of God is a matter of representing the incarnately human, crucified and risen Jesus Christ (not just the earthly 'male' Jesus) to his people. The acceptance of women as ministers today, while it may be in contrast to the *cultural* norms of

New Testament times, is perfectly consistent with the *theological* thrust of the apostolic faith, and indeed, may well lead us to a deeper understanding of what that ministry comprises and entails.

With baptism, many Baptists would argue, the case is far different: infant baptism, which becomes characteristic of post-Constantinian Christianity, was not just a different form of administration of baptism, but with it went a quite different theology from that of the New Testament. No longer was it the point at which human response met the divine initiative through personal identification and union with the death and resurrection of Jesus Christ; instead it became the means by which 'grace' in a less than personal sense was dispensed, a development of tradition which in fact obscured the apostolic teaching and practice.

Beneath both these answers two poles are held in tension: faithfulness to the apostolic norm, and readiness to let the apostolic intent find appropriate new expression for new contexts and so create a new spurt of tradition. It was thus not entirely paradoxical, for example, that while the first few generations of Baptists were rigorously opposed to allowing any set words other than those of scripture in their worship, and refused to allow anything but psalms to be sung, it was among the Baptists and their Independent kinsfolk of the later seventeenth century that hymns for congregational use arose, and one of the most enriching traditions of Christian worship in these islands was born. Faithfulness to the apostolic faith in scripture was met by the demand to give it voice in new tongues.

What holds the two poles in tension is an underlying belief as to what the whole exercise is about: mission. The apostles were those who were *sent into the world*, not just elevated to safe niches to be venerated for all time; apostolicity means engaging today in the continuance of that mission in the power of the Spirit. It does not mean a sterile attempt to preserve unchanged what is thought to have been 'at the beginning'. It means the dynamic missionary venture to witness to what will be 'at the end', and is now already coming to be, the lordship of Christ over all people and all creation. Between these poles and in this missionary tension Baptists will not be ashamed of a certain pragmatism, expressed well by a scholar of a former generation, H. Wheeler Robinson: 'Is there any test of methods of organization and government save that they should be the best to promote the faith and service of the Gospel?'[32]

Within churches and denominations, traditions tend to cluster around definitive individuals in their history. Among Baptists none is of greater significance than William Carey, effectively the pioneer of the western Protestant missionary enterprise. Carey's famous *Enquiry* of 1792 is justly regarded as the charter of the new missionary age. It can also, however, be read as a classic case of the Baptist approach to tradition. At the heart of its theological argument is the claim that the 'great commission' of Matthew 28.18–20 applies no less to the church of the present than to the first apostles. In reading it thus, Carey was subverting centuries of tradition – including nearly two centuries of Baptist tradition – which had interpreted it merely as a historical account of the charge to those apostles. Accepted belief and practice were being critically scrutinized in the light of a re-reading of the scriptures, a re-reading stimulated of course by certain developments in the religious social and political context of the time. Tradition, secondary to scripture, was being recognized for what it was. But also, in the light of that recovery of the biblical imperative, a new and positive reading of much else in the tradition took place. In fact there was a wholesale retrieval of elements in the Christian past which for long had been unknown or neglected by Protestants – the earlier missionary tradition of the church. Hence a substantial part of the *Enquiry* consists of a historical overview – and an ecumenical one at that

– of earlier missionary enterprises from the first centuries through the middle ages until Carey's own day.

By distinguishing the word of God in scripture from tradition, not only is the distinctiveness of the 'apostolic faith' kept in view. Tradition itself is preserved and revivified for its best uses in the mission of the people of God. That, it is to be hoped, will provide a Baptist motivation and contribution in the continuing ecumenical pilgrimage.

A METHODIST VIEW
Rupert E. Davies

John Wesley refused to think of himself and his followers as separated, or separating, from the Church of England. 'I live and die a member of the Church of England,' he announced in his later years, and he held that church to be the best-ordered church in Christendom. He sometimes embarked on courses of action – such as preaching in other men's parishes without permission, and, especially, ordaining to the priesthood – which seemed to his critics, and to his brother Charles, to give the lie to his protestations, but there is no doubt that he adhered to them until the end of his life.

In accordance with this he constantly claimed that the doctrines which he taught were the doctrines of the Church of England, in complete conformity with the Thirty-Nine Articles of that church, and with the Homilies which expound them. He held that its bishops and other teachers had allowed many of their church's doctrines to fall into desuetude, and made it his business to reaffirm them. These 'neglected' doctrines included that of Redemption through Christ, Justification by Faith, the Witness of the Spirit as giving assurance of salvation, and the call to seek Perfect Love (or 'Entire Sanctification'). These were all, he claimed, within the liturgical and theological framework of the Book of Common Prayer, the Articles and the Homilies.

So, while others might question his loyalty to Anglican orthodoxy, he himself had no doubts in his own mind on this point; indeed he felt free to doubt the orthodoxy – sometimes justly – of certain bishops and deans, as well as of ordinary clergy.

His claims in this matter stand up well to examination. Some Anglican eyebrows may be lifted in relation to 'assurance of salvation' and 'perfect love' (especially if it is called 'entire sanctification'). But it has to be remembered that zeal and commitment were at a low ebb in the Anglicanism of his time, and that he was therefore inclined, understandably, to over-emphasize, and even to exaggerate, teachings about inward religion which were undoubtedly biblical and Anglican, but seemed to him to have gone by default.

When it came to his teaching about tradition, therefore, we cannot expect him to propose a view which he believed to be other than a genuinely Anglican one, nor did he. Later developments in Anglicanism, such as the Oxford Movement, which successfully promulgated a view of tradition very different from Wesley's, have obscured this fact, but fact it remains. Wesley's doctrine of tradition was Anglican long before it was Methodist, and it may be suspected that in general outline, at least, it has persisted in some Anglican circles to the present day.

Wesley leaves no doubt in anyone's mind that he regarded the Bible as the supreme source of Christian truth, possessing absolute authority. The scriptures are the 'oracles of God'; they are given by the Holy Spirit. No one and nothing can stand above them or alongside them. 'God himself has condescended to teach the way (of salvation); for this very end he came down from heaven. He hath written it down in a book. O give me that book! At any price give me the Book of God!'[1]

He thus claims that his whole theology comes from the Bible, and that if anyone wishes to controvert his teaching, he must bring evidence for his different view from the Bible, or Wesley will not give him a hearing.

It is the whole Bible, not selections from it, that he here sets up in absolute supremacy. So, if in his reading of the Bible he finds a 'dark or intricate' passage, whose meaning is open to doubt, he asserts that the right course for the puzzled reader is first of all to pray to God for enlightenment, and then to 'search after and consider parallel passages of Scripture, "comparing spiritual things with spiritual" '.[2]

So great and constant is his insistence on the supreme authority of scripture that it would be easy to suppose that he had no use for tradition at all, since everything that is needed for the salvation and enlightenment of humankind is already supplied by God without it. Some of his followers, indeed, have taken this to be his position, and proceeded to discard all tradition as a human invention.

But this is not Wesley's view. His acceptance of the Anglican Articles and Homilies, which must be classed as tradition, has been already noted. And in the very passage just quoted about the God-given character of scripture, he goes on to say that if after comparison with parallel passages the meaning of the passage in question remains doubtful, he proceeds to 'consult those who are experienced in the things of God, and then the writings whereby, being dead, they yet speak'.

We have quickly reached the core of his doctrine of tradition: it is subservient to scripture, but highly useful for the elucidation of scripture. Within tradition he gave the foremost place to the wisdom of the Fathers; they are 'the most authentic Commentators on Scripture, as being both nearest the fountain and eminently endued with that Spirit by whom "all Scripture was given" '.[3]

He venerated chiefly the Ante-Nicene Fathers, but he also praised Gregory of Nyssa,[4] Chrysostom,[5] Basil,[6] Jerome,[7] Augustine,[8] the Egyptian Macarius,[9] and Ephraem the Syrian.[10] He especially admired the last-named for his insight into the devotional life. He is silent about post-Chalcedonian theologians and has little respect for the Schoolmen; he regarded the

Council of Trent as lamentably confused on Justification and Sanctification, and as having aimed its doctrinal thrusts at the Church of England. He of course applauded the Continental Reformation, but he does not esteem Luther and Calvin as biblical expositors so very highly, since Luther misunderstood the Bible on the subject of holiness, and Calvin favoured the obnoxious doctrine of predestination; these men certainly threw light on the scriptures after many centuries of darkness, but he is careful to say that they also, like all other expositors, must be judged by the touchstone of scripture.

The list of writers who 'being dead, yet speak' in authentic tones is completed by the names of those who in addition to those already mentioned, appear in the *Christian Library*, which Wesley published (with some consequent financial loss) for the spiritual and theological benefit of his followers in 1749. Fifty authors find a place in this series of volumes, and it is not to be supposed that Wesley ascribed equal authority to all of them. But the variety of schools of thought manifested in his choice shows how deep was his respect for those who interpreted the scriptures in an illuminating way, whatever their denomination.

Here are some of the authors: Joseph and Richard Alleine (Puritans), Samuel Annesley (Puritan), Isaac Barrow (Anglican), Richard Baxter (Presbyterian), Antoinette Bourignon (mystical ex-Roman Catholic), John Bunyan (Baptist/Independent), Ralph Cudworth (Anglican Platonist), Archbishop Fénelon (Roman Catholic Quietist), Anthony Horneck (of the Religious Societies), Bishop Ken (Anglican), Michael Molinos (Roman Catholic Quietist), Henry More (Anglican Platonist), John Owen (Independent), Emil Pascal (Roman Catholic Jansenist), Samuel Rutherford (Presbyterian) and Archbishop Tillotson (Anglican) – together with a further group of Fathers; Clement of Rome,[11] Polycarp,[12] and Ignatius,[13] and the Protestant *par excellence*, John Foxe[14] (*The Acts and Monuments of the Christian Martyrs*). The absence of Martin Luther and John Calvin from the *Library* is notable.

To all these commentators and exegetes we must add the Articles and Homilies whose place in tradition he can be said to take for granted.

The most conspicuous example of the way in which he put his beliefs about tradition into practice is his 'setting apart' of one man, already an ordained priest (or presbyter) as Superintendent, and his ordination of two others as ministers of word and sacrament. The setting apart and the ordinations were carried out for the benefit of the Methodists in America, and they were followed by a few ordinations for Scotland and England. He was quite sure at all times that the New Testament laid down no pattern of ministerial order, and that therefore the threefold ministry of bishops, priests and deacons was not mandatory. The ordering of each church was therefore indicated by tradition: that is, it sprang ultimately from a particular *interpretation* of scripture, and needed to be in accordance with scripture; but it was not laid down as a prescription from scripture. It came, in fact, in the category of 'opinions', not basic doctrines. For Wesley taught that there was a great variety of 'opinions', including many of those held by the Church of Rome, none of which made Christian fellowship impossible between those who thought differently.[15]

On these grounds he fully approved the ordering of the Church of England, although he did not grant it scriptural authority, and although he maintained that the 'uninterrupted succession' of bishops was 'a fable which no man ever did or can prove'. He also held at the same time the accepted Protestant view that the true succession of divinely appointed and assisted pastors and teachers was maintained in the Reformed Churches on the Continent and in Scotland and England.

In the light of these long-held convictions it is not surprising that he came to be persuaded by the Anglican writers Lord Peter

King[16] and Bishop Stillingfleet[17] that (*a*) according to scripture bishops and presbyters are the same order (though different in degree), (*b*) presbyters have an inherent right to perform the office of a bishop, and (*c*) they are entitled to do so with their bishop's permission (King) or, in case of necessity, without it (Stillingfleet).[18] These authors, in effect, he accepted as good tradition, though in conflict, no doubt, with other traditions in the Church of England.

But so great was his respect for the ordering of the Church of England, and so strong was his desire not to do anything which would cause or accelerate separation from that church, that he refrained for forty years from putting into effect what he had learned from these two mentors. Eventually, after the War of Independence, when there were about 15,000 Methodists in America without anyone of their number to administer to them the sacrament of Holy Communion (and very few Anglican priests, in case by any chance they were willing to accept their ministrations), he judged that the 'necessity' had now come (though not his bishop's permission). He therefore ordained two of his preachers as presbyters in Bristol in 1784; and for good measure, and the administration of the Methodist societies in America, he 'set apart' Thomas Coke, an ordained priest of the Church of England, as 'Superintendent'. The other ordinations by Wesley which followed, about twenty-seven in number, were also justified by the plea of 'necessity' (usually in the form of the parish priest's idleness and dereliction of duty).

There is one use of language which might suggest that Wesley went beyond Anglican doctrine. To this day every ordained Methodist minister is required to reply once a year to the questions: 'Do you believe and preach our doctrines, and will you administer our discipline?' (the consequences of a negative answer are not specified). The phrase 'our doctrines' goes back to Wesley, and might seem to be a claim on his part to have discovered, or to have had revealed to him, certain doctrines unknown to the rest of the church. If this were the case, Wesley would indeed be asserting that the Methodism had found a new and authentic interpretation of scripture which ranked with those of the early Fathers. But it is not the case. In this rather surprising phrase Wesley was simply making his usual claim to have recovered certain tenets of biblical faith which had been forgotten or neglected, in line with his attempt to restore primitive Christianity within the Church of England.

Wesley, then, gave the highest place to scripture, as the fountain of truth, and the second place to tradition, as the interpreter of scripture. He also set much store by reason and religious experience, but in a different context.

He was in many ways the child of his age, the Age of Reason. It was never for him the task of reason to discover or reveal the truth; but reason was useful as the servant of what we have called tradition in comparing interpretation with interpretation, in confuting false interpretations and in defending biblical faith by argument. He addressed several published 'Appeals' to 'Men of Reason and Religion', and was himself no mean practitioner of rational argument according to the logic which prevailed in his time. It is not surprising that his object in the education provided at Kingswood School, his favourite institution, was to produce 'rational, scriptural Christians'.

He was concerned with religious experience mainly in the forms which it took in the life of Methodists. At first he was impressed by the 'extraordinary manifestations' which were provoked by his early preaching to unlettered crowds; but he always slightly mistrusted them (though he believed them to be validated, when authentic, by the New Testament), and came to distrust them more and more. They do not find a place in his mature theological thought, though he could not discount them completely. But he firmly believed that to those who trusted in Christ for salvation God normally (he at first said 'always', but he retracted this) granted 'assurance' – an 'inward impression of the soul' that they were children of God. This was described biblically in the words: 'The spirit itself beareth witness with our spirit that we are the children of God' (Rom. 8.16 AV), and was confirmed for the believer and those who observed this way of life by peace of mind, joy and love. But this experience was never used by Wesley to establish or demonstrate a doctrine, even though in the early days of his ministry he regarded its presence or absence as the test of genuine faith, and applied this test to himself.

In the nineteenth and early twentieth centuries in England,[19] not least in the Wesleyan Methodist Church, the largest of the Methodist bodies, his successors as teachers of the Methodists failed, except in rare cases, to maintain his careful ordering of the relative places of scripture, tradition, reason and experience. Indeed, there was a strong tendency to leave tradition and reason on one side, and to pass straight from scripture to experience, encouraging critics to say that Methodists believed in salvation by feeling. Experience, in fact, in some Methodist circles came close to becoming a source of truth in its own right.[20] This was no doubt due to the indirect influence of Friedrich Schleiermacher, with his concept of religion as a 'feeling of dependence'. But a stronger cause was the rise of Tractarianism (followed by the birth of Anglo-Catholicism), with its contempt for Methodists and for their notion of personal salvation, and its canonization of the early Fathers as the pillar and ground of the truth. In reaction, methodist thinkers brought out the evidence from personal experience, and indicated that respect for tradition could lead straight to Rome, as in the case of John Henry Newman. It may be also that the Methodists were so preoccupied with creating and developing their own institutions (including the constitution and supremacy of the Conference), to meet the needs of the times, that the appeal to tradition had little force.

The first stirring of ecumenism in the 1920s and the need to prepare for the reunion of the three main branches of British Methodism, scheduled for 1932, produced a fresh interest in the theology of Wesley. This was also the time when Methodist teachers, after a period of theological isolation, were subjected once again to the influence of non-Methodist writings – ancient, Reformation and modern – and were drawing the attention of their students to the advances in biblical scholarship in which Methodists were playing a leading part.

For legal and other purposes the representatives of the uniting Methodist churches in the 1920s hammered out a 'Deed of Union' which was to form the basis of the Methodist Church Union Act which Parliament passed in 1929. Included in the Deed of Union, by common consent, were the 'Doctrinal Clauses', accepted by all, and declared unalterable except by Act of Parliament. The formulation of these Doctrinal Clauses was preceded, of course, by much theological argument between those who spoke for the three branches of Methodism. And the final formulation of the Clauses bears all the marks of painful achievement by a committee. Unfortunately, also, the Clauses are framed in the stilted and unpunctuated language required by lawyers. Even so, they express the convictions about scripture and tradition, as about other matters, which were widely held at the time of Methodist Union. They are an integral part of the charter document of the Methodist Church, and are indeed the only formal statement of its doctrines.[21]

Yet it is not an easy or uncontroversial task to set out in precise terms their teaching on the various topics which they touch, and their statements on scripture and tradition are not exempt from this difficulty. What follows, however, might well gain the support of most Methodists who have given thought to the matter.

The first paragraph claims for Methodism a 'place in the Holy Catholic Church', and this affirms from the outset the right of the Methodist Church, which it shares with the other churches, to participation in the development and acceptance of the history of the universal church through the ages. That is to say, the saints and martyrs and teachers of all the churches, together with the inheritance of devotion, liturgy and learning which they have handed down, belong as truly to the Methodist Church as to any other part of the Holy Catholic Church. St Francis of Assisi, for instance, is not to be seen as a Roman Catholic, nor Richard Hooker (at any rate, primarily) as an Anglican, but both are representatives of the tradition which is common to us all, in spite of our divisions.

The paragraph goes on to specify certain elements in that tradition, after the mention of the apostolic faith which is enshrined in scripture. It asserts loyal acceptance of the 'fundamental principles of the historic creeds and the Protestant Reformation'. The 'historic creeds' must be the Apostles' and Nicene Creeds, and, presumably, the Chalcedonian Definition. It is in this way that the place in tradition of the ante- and post-Nicene Fathers, together with the creeds produced on the basis of their teaching, is acknowledged. But there is a conspicuous absence of reference to the theologians of the Dark and Middle Ages, such as Anselm and the Schoolmen. There is a jump straight from Chalcedon to Martin Luther.

It is not made clear what is meant by the Protestant Reformation. Is the English Reformation included under this title? Probably the nub of the answer is, according to received views in Methodism at the time, that the work of Martin Luther and John Calvin, and perhaps Ulrich Zwingli, is intended (though we have referred earlier to John Wesley's view of Luther and Calvin). Yet the features of the English Reformation that were conformable with the teachings of the Continental Reformers may also have been in mind.

But what is meant by the 'fundamental principles' of the historic creeds and the Protestant Reformation? This question has never been officially answered by the Methodist Church. The creeds could well be said to consist of nothing but fundamental principles, so that the phrase is odd. Perhaps we can say that the fundamental principles of the creeds form what remains in the Nicene Creed and the Chalcedonian Definition after the technical terminology (derived from the philosophical schools of the time) has been stripped away,[22] and the underlying meaning uncovered.

When the same question is asked about the Protestant Reformation, the answer is equally hard to find, but for a different reason. Scholars of different Reformed communions, and within these communions, come up with different statements of the 'fundamental principles'. Secular historians have even suggested that 'the right to private judgment' should be included (which would have greatly surprised the Reformers). It is perhaps best to say that these 'principles' are quite widely agreed to be: the supremacy of scripture, the unmerited grace of God, justification by grace through faith in Jesus Christ, the priesthood of all believers, the guidance and power of the Holy Spirit, and the obligatory celebration of the sacraments of Baptism and Holy Communion (some of these appear explicitly in later Doctrinal Clauses).

The beliefs of Methodism are then summed up as 'the Evangelical Faith', and this faith is declared in the second paragraph to be based upon 'the Divine revelation recorded in holy scriptures'. This revelation is to be the supreme rule of faith and practice. No explicit mention is made of tradition in the form of scriptural interpretation, but is certainly implied that all tradition is to be tested by the touchstone of scripture. Or rather, by the 'divine revelation recorded in scripture', which tells strongly against a literalist understanding of scripture, and leaves the door open for critical scholarship to follow its proper procedures.

But now the paragraph makes an addition to the content of tradition as it was understood until the time of Wesley. The

'Evangelical Doctrines', of Methodism, it states, are 'contained in' (not 'laid down by') Wesley's *Notes on the New Testament* and the first four volumes of his sermons (as published at the time of the Deed).[23] But it is clear from the next paragraph that this addition to tradition is not a body of new truth, revealed to the Methodists, but an elucidation of the scriptures by Wesley which was deemed helpful for the understanding of the gospel.

The next paragraph indicates the purpose which the *Notes on the New Testament* and the *Sermons* are intended to serve, which is not 'to impose a system of formal or speculative theology', but 'to set up standards of belief and preaching which should secure loyalty to the fundamental truths of the Gospel of Redemption'.

The word 'standards', which is also used in the title of the whole series of Doctrinal Clauses, is, no doubt, carefully chosen, but it is not easy to define. It is plainly not used in the educational sense of 'a target set up for achievement'. Rather, it means a norm by which the believing and preaching of Methodists are to be judged. There is also perhaps in the use of the word something of what modern people mean by parameters, limits beyond which it is not proper for Methodist preachers to go. It has to be frankly admitted that the designation of the *Notes on the New Testament* as a standard causes considerable difficulties. In the first place, they are rarely read, even by those who are required to read them – and, when read, rarely quoted. In the second place, they are based to a large extent on the work of Johannes Bengel, a Lutheran scholar of the first part of the eighteenth century. He was a pioneer of textual criticism, and his *Gnomon Novi Testamenti* is rightly regarded as a classic of early modern New Testament scholarship. But his methods and conclusions have now been largely superseded, and Wesley's version of his exegesis has certainly an uneasy and insecure place in tradition (this is why it is, for the most part, tacitly disregarded).

The case of the *Forty-Four Sermons* is different. No one could be expected to accept every statement in them, and some of the New Testament exegesis which they contain is, as we in our time would have to say, plainly wrong. But there is no doubt that the 'fundamental principles' of Wesley's 'Evangelical Faith' are 'contained in' them. Therefore they stand firm in tradition as Methodists conceive it, and in recent years many scholars, after a period of academic disdain, have borne witness to the validity, though not the absolute truth, of their theology.

The next five paragraphs concern themselves with the doctrine of the Christian ministry, lay and ordained. They bear many marks, as one would expect, of prolonged debate between those with a 'high' doctrine of the ordained ministry, and those with a lower one – very roughly, 'Wesleyan' and 'Primitive'. They cannot be said to solve all the problems about the ministry which were current at the time of their formulation; still less, those which have arisen since. But the general sense which emerges can be set down in a few sentences:

Christians belong to the priesthood of all believers. There is no other priesthood – certainly not one differing in kind from this priesthood. The ministers of Christ, lay and ordained, within the priesthood, are stewards of the household of God, the church; and some of them have this as their sole occupation and play a leading role in spiritual matters. These are the ordained ministers, who are called by God, endowed by him with the necessary gifts and graces, and ordained by the laying-on-of-hands to express the church's recognition of their call. Both lay and ordained ministers are examined and tested before they exercise their ministry. Ordained ministers are set apart by their ordination to the ministry of word and sacraments for the sake of church order. In all this the principle of representative selection is observed.

The last paragraph of all in the Clauses insists on Baptism and the Lord's Supper as divine institutions and Christian obligations, and this indicates clearly that the gospel sacraments belong to the essence of the Methodist Church.

However pleased the authors of these Clauses may have been with the result of their work, and however warmly the first conference of the re-united Methodist Church in 1932 may have endorsed them, it soon became clear that they were by no means free from ambiguity, and even contained unresolved inconsistencies. But the Deed of Union had wisely added to the Doctrinal Clauses a provision that 'the Conference shall be the final authority within the Methodist Church with regard to all questions concerning the interpretation of its doctrines'. Thus the annual Conference, consisting of an equal number of laypeople and ordained ministers, was constituted as the guardian and interpreter of Methodist faith, and in fact its agent for the transmission of tradition.

This task it has normally discharged by requesting its Faith and Order Committee to investigate matters of interpretation brought to its notice, and to submit a report in due course. Since 1932 many such reports have been submitted and adopted; and have thus become the Conference's interpretation of Methodist doctrines.[24]

Chief among these pronouncements of the Conference have been those on 'the nature of the church according to the scriptures', on baptism and church membership, and, most frequent of all, on ordination and on lay and ordained ministries. In the last regard, the 'priesthood of all believers', the 'principle of representative selection', the 'leading role' of the ordained ministry, the meaning of 'sole occupation', and, in recent years, the role of lay ministry, have all come up for careful investigation. Those who have read through all the documents thus accumulated as doctrinal resolutions of Conference are agreed that there has been a steady and consistent development in the

46

interpretation of the ideas contained in the Doctrinal Clauses, and that this is true not least of those on the ordained ministry.

In summary we may now conclude that the Methodist doctrine of tradition, as officially stated or implied, is that, under the supreme control of the revelation of God in scripture, the role of tradition is to clarify, expound and interpret that revelation; and that tradition is to be found in the historic creeds, the writings of the continental Reformers, and, for Methodists (and anyone else who comes to accept it) in certain published writings of John Wesley, in the Doctrinal Clauses of the Deed of Union and in the interpretation of the Clauses announced from time to time by the Methodist Conference.

It is to be carefully noticed that there is no hint that tradition is infallible, or that it is now complete; or that there is no other source of tradition than those just mentioned.

Since 1932 the Methodist Church, like all other churches, has been opened up to new and powerful pressures and influences both from within its own ranks and from outside itself. Many of these pressures and influences have been theological and have required considerable adaptability from Methodism's leaders and teachers. In general the response of these people has been positive and constructive, though a few of them have reacted against the revolutionary temper of the times and retreated into a laager mentality, crying 'Wesley, the whole Wesley, and nothing but Wesley'. Not surprisingly, several of the issues that have been raised are directly relevant to the matter of tradition.

First and foremost, there has been a steady advance in biblical scholarship, and certain hitherto suspected facts have now been established by its methods: for instance, (*a*) there are the seeds of several theologies, not just one, in the New Testament, and those theologies are not wholly consistent with each other; (*b*) the synoptic Gospels can no longer be taken as giving an accurate account of the words and deeds of Jesus, but rather represent the teaching and preaching of the Early Church *about* Jesus, based, of course, on the recollections, some of them written down, some not, of eye-witnesses and their disciples; and then edited and published in various Christian centres for the benefit of converts; and (*c*) that the Fourth Gospel is a theological, not an historical book, for the most part consisting of prolonged meditations on the significance of what Jesus was, did and said, in the light of what the churches had come to believe about him. Simplistic statements, such as 'the Bible says', are now ruled out; and we cannot quote the Fourth Gospel as giving the actual words of Jesus.

Then the development of ecumenism has plunged Methodism into innumerable conversations with Christians of other churches, in Britain and across the world, both in the somewhat rarefied atmosphere of the Faith and Order Movement of the World Council of Churches, and in local and national consultations with a view to Christian unity. This has led Methodism to the understanding and appreciation of other theological convictions than its own; of similarities of belief between itself and other communions, long concealed by differences of terminology and ways of thought; and of its own place in the total spectrum of catholicity. These discoveries have been crystallized in the Anglican-Methodist Reports of the fifties and sixties, and in Roman Catholic-Methodist reports since then, and they have made themselves felt in many experiments in unity on the local scene.

The effects on Methodism of this ecumenical engagement have been numerous and profound (this is why the new ecumenical slogan 'Not Strangers but Pilgrims' strikes Methodists as slightly odd; it is a long time since Methodists were strangers to other Christians). There has been a notable development in the understanding of the Christian life as corporate, that is, in the doctrine of the church, to be set alongside the continued Methodist emphasis on the value to God of each individual person. There has been a growth also in the sense of the church as continuous in time as well as universal in scope. There has been an increase in eucharistic practice and an enhancement of sacramental doctrine. The liturgy of Methodism has been reviewed and revised in close association with other beneficiaries of the Liturgical Movement. At the same time, by contrast but not in opposition, Methodism has become more aware of its own identity, helped in this by the quinquennial 'Oxford Theological Institute', where American and British theologians have met each other, and both have met the representatives of Methodism from the Third World.

It has to be acknowledged that in some quarters the individualism which was characteristic of nineteenth-century teaching and practice, with its concentration on private virtues and their somewhat materialistic rewards, lingers on; and also that the Anglican rejections of union have sent some Methodists back into pre-ecumenical ways of thinking. But there is good reason to believe that time and the new ecumenism will reverse these tendencies.

Involvement in the Methodist churches of Africa, Australia, Asia and the Caribbean, nearly all now autonomous, and in the united churches of South and North India, has brought home to Methodists in Britain the dissatisfaction of many non-Western Christians with the formulae of Christian belief which have been accepted in Europe for two thousand years. All of these, it is said, reflect concepts and ideas about the world, its creator and its inhabitants, which betray a purely Western interpretation of the scriptures; and not only the formulae, but some of the items of faith, such as some doctrines of the Atonement, fail to make any sense in Eastern or African ears. Hence the growth of Indian and Black Theologies, which sometimes seem startlingly different from what British Methodists have been taught to believe.

And there is the arrival of Liberation Theology from Latin

America. According to this, the real emphasis of the New Testament, which is on the total liberation of peoples and people, has been watered down in Europe and the United States to a pietistic gospel of personal salvation, agreeable to capitalist and colonialist societies; and the statements of Jesus about good news to the poor and freeing of the captives have been spiritualized beyond recognition.

A particular form of Liberation Theology has been shaped and defended by Christian Feminists; and this has now taken firm roots in American and British theology. It could be summed up like this: 'The Bible and acres upon acres of Christian theology were written by men, largely with men in mind. Between them the authors have, consciously or unconsciously, suppressed, or in other cases distorted, the original teaching and practice of Jesus. But they have failed in the end to conceal the fact that Jesus made absolutely no discrimination between men and women. Therefore we need to see the Gospel afresh through the eyes and minds of women; and, if we do, new statements of it will appear.' They already do.

Then, the methods of sociology have been at last applied to church history, and not least to the growth of tradition. It is now hard to deny that cultural, political and economic forces have played a great part in fashioning (some would even say, creating) doctrines and practices in all parts of the church. Was not the institution (and even the apparel) of episcopacy moulded, or maybe created, on the model of the provincial government of the Roman Empire? The Papacy on the model of the semi-divine Emperor? Were the creeds not formulated in the language and thought of contemporary philosophy? Were not the churches of the Reformation impelled into existence by the rise of the nation-state and the new commercial classes? Was not the Methodist Revival invigorated by the frustrations and aspirations of the English working classes, and its later structure adapted to their needs? Was not the Tractarian doctrine of the

Apostolic Succession thought up, and traced back to the writings of the Fathers, because of the need to resist the erosion of the sacred office of bishop by liberalism and secularism in the nineteenth century?

The presence in strength of non-Christian faiths in Britain, with their clearly articulated basic beliefs, traditions and customs has raised in an acute form the question of the finality of Christianity. Can we still affirm the statement of the Johannine Jesus: 'No one comes to the Father, but by me'? Can we go on with evangelism as before?

We should perhaps add the controversial contentions of David Jenkins about the Virgin Birth and the Resurrection. But these have caused nothing like the same disturbance in the Methodist Church as in the Church of England, since the questions raised by Bishop Jenkins were already very familiar in Methodism, and had been peaceably discussed for a long time. On the other hand, the view of Don Cupitt, that Christians ought now to have passed the stage of believing in a personal God, has not, perhaps because of its apparent sophistication, impinged very much on the Methodist consciousness.

But certainly we must add the burgeoning study of 'ecotheology', the theology of the environment, though its findings are as yet far from clear.

Taken together, these various developments, though the impact of some has been much greater than that of others, amount to a formidable bombardment of traditional teaching. On the whole, the Doctrinal Clauses of the Deed of Union, as interpreted and supported by subsequent resolutions of the Methodist Conference, together with the doctrine of tradition that they state or imply, have stood up well. The upholders of the Clauses have not shied away from disturbing ideas, but claimed that some of such truths as have been recently unearthed can be included with the generous scope of the Methodist 'standards', since they present themselves as interpretations of scripture which the church must judge to be valid or not; while the rest purport to spring from the activity of the Holy Spirit as he guides the church into all the truth.

But the defence and the claim can be, and have been, called into question in recent years; and it seems inherently unlikely that the formulations of 1932 will wholly satisfy the church of the twenty-first century. So perhaps the time has come to enquire whether a new view of tradition in particular will better meet the demands of the scriptural and historical knowledge that we now possess.

The Fourth World Conference of Faith and Order, held in Montreal in 1963, gave particular attention to the question of tradition, and submitted to the churches a report on the subject which included the statement quoted more fully by Keith Clements on p. 17:

Our starting point is that we are all living in a tradition which goes back to our Lord and has its roots in the Old Testament, and are all indebted to that tradition inasmuch as we have received the revealed truth, the Gospel, through its being transmitted from one generation to another. Thus we can say that we exist as Christians by the Tradition of the Gospel, testified in Scripture, transmitted in and by the Church, through the power of the Holy Spirit.[25]

This not entirely clear statement and the report of which it is a part have certainly entered the thinking of many theologians, but there is no sign that they have greatly affected the theological life of the churches. What now follows as a personal proposal is by no means a reproduction of the report as a whole, but it is influenced by it.

I begin by casting serious doubt on the sharp distinction between scripture and tradition in the early writings of the church which has been habitual since the Reformation and before it. This distinction has meant that all the books within the canon of the New Testament, and none but these, are scripture; all other early Christian literature, if it is valued at all, is tradition. But the truth is that the Epistle of Jude, the Second Epistle of Peter, the Second and Third Epistles of John, and (some would say) the Pastoral Epistles, the Epistle of James and the Apocalypse of John, have no obvious superiority to the *Didache*, the *Epistle to the Corinthians* of Clement of Rome, and the *Shepherd* of Hermas. Why is the first set of books included in the New Testament, and the second not? Only, so far as we can tell, because apostolic authorship was ascribed to those in the first set, and not to those in the second (it must be admitted that if the *Shepherd* had been included, the New Testament would be a good deal longer than it is). But we now know, with virtual certainty, that such apostolic ascription was wrongly made – that no apostle had anything personally to do with the writing of the books in the first set; they remain in the New Testament by the power of tradition alone, embodied in a decree of the Council of Nicaea in 323 AD.

The conventional distinction therefore is hard to defend, and this is so even if we limit scripture to the undoubtedly 'apostolic' books – the Gospels, the Acts, the authentic writings of Paul, the Epistle to the Hebrews, the First Epistle of Peter and the First Epistle of John; we cannot sharply distinguish even these from tradition. For, although the word 'apostolic' can truly be applied to them, in the sense that they were written in substance either by an apostle or under the direct influence of an apostle (and probably while some of the apostles were still alive), all of them, except for the Epistles of Paul and the First Epistle of Peter, and perhaps some of these, contain elements which seem to belong to an age after that of the apostles and which would be categorized as tradition if they appeared in other writings – the Birth and Infancy narratives in the First and Third Gospels, for instance, some of the miracles in the First Gospel, and the long discourses in the Fourth Gospel. Each of these examples can no doubt be disputed, but at least it will be agreed that the passages referred to have a different flavour from the narratives which can be recognized as directly derived from those who personally participated in the events to which they refer, that is, from the apostles.

It is, in fact, my contention that a distinction so hard to draw should be abolished altogether. It was a false, though well-intentioned, distinction in the first place. And the abolition can be carried out without disrespect to either scripture or tradition, as we shall see, lest the champions of either be afraid that we are reaching a purely negative standpoint.

Let us state the position in a different way. Tradition in the simplest sense consists in what has been handed down from the past into the present. In the Christian sense it is 'the Gospel, testified in Scripture, transmitted in and by the church, through the power of the Holy Spirit'.[26] This definition points the way forward, and we can say:

Tradition begins with the story of Abraham's call, and continues with the accounts of the formation of the People of God through the Mosaic covenant, and of the frequent falls from grace of that People, and with the assertion of God's judgment and the promise of redemption in the writings of the prophets. It reaches its climax in the evangelists' narratives of the coming of Christ, the interpretation of that event by the apostles, and the description of the new life in Christ within the new People of God. Then it goes on in the explication of the gospel and the Christian life to meet the needs and answer the questions of each succeeding generation; and will continue so till the end of time.

From the earliest years it is to be found, not only in formal writings, but also in liturgies and prayers and hymns, in scholarly and devotional treatises, in occasional writings and sermons, in confessions of faith, and in the biographies of martyrs and saints.

It is open-ended and never complete or final. It is, in fact, the 'living stream of the church's life'.[27]

If this is so, scripture is part of tradition, and not distinct from it. But not an ordinary part. It must be the affirmation of the Christian church that, on the contrary, it is the determinative, the all-important part, since it prepares for and centres in the incarnation of the Son of God, and it contains our earliest, primary and essential witness to the Gospel. It can be called 'tradition *par excellence*'. By it all the claims of other works to authentic tradition are judged.

But not all of it, or every word and passage in it. We have seen that tradition passes from one stage to another within the pages of the New Testament itself, though argument will no doubt continue as to which writings embody the climactic and primary stage and which the secondary stage, of the transmission of the gospel. Martin Luther held that the criterion of apostolicity lay in the doctrine of justification by faith as expounded in the Epistle to the Romans; we should rather affirm that the primary stage is found in the Gospels, the Acts and the undoubted Epistles of Paul, together with the Epistle to the Ephesians and the First Epistles of John and Peter, and that the criterion of gospel truth is provided by these books. Wherever we draw the line, however, it is clear that the next stage of Christian tradition is reached in certain New Testament writings (such as the Epistle of James) and continues in the *Didache*, the *Shepherd* and the *Epistle of Clement*, written in all likelihood before the last book of the New Testament (II Peter in all probability) was published.

The list of places where tradition is to be found in post-New Testament times is bound to include the following: the writings of the Fathers (or some of them), the historic creeds, the *Summae* of the Schoolmen, the classic liturgies of the Eastern and Western churches, the Confessions of the Churches of the Reformation, the Articles of the Church of England, the testimonies of the Society of Friends, the Sermons of John Wesley, the Doctrinal Clauses of the Methodist Deed of Union (and similar pronouncements of other churches), and the Barmen Declaration of the German Confessing Church. There are, and will be, many other candidates for inclusion.

We do well also to add to our list the protestations of small groups of believers on the fringes of the institutional churches, and sometimes within those churches, which have continued the tradition in idiosyncratic ways, finding the 'orthodox' ways rigid and sterile, and feeling themselves called to rebel against them.

It is clear from this list that tradition is found in varied and sometimes contradictory forms. The variations arise from many different causes. The tendency of the 'sub-apostolic' form to equate the gospel with a new law springs from the need to counter the immorality of pagan religion and to indicate the relation of the Christian church to Judaism. The denigration of sex, and with it the degradation of women, which are traceable in parts of the New Testament, and become vigorous soon after New Testament times, and recur for many centuries, come partly from Gnostic views of the evil of matter and partly from some assumptions of Greek philosophy, encouraged by certain Pauline passages (while others are neglected).

Mediaeval writings reflect the feudal temper of the age and the rediscovery of the long-lost writings of Aristotle. Reformation authors in their rejection of the Pope and all his thoughts and works are partly influenced by the emergence of nation states and overseas trade, Methodist doctrine by the alienation from the Church of England of those considered incapable of grasping the gospel, the Barmen Declaration by the Weltanschauung of Nazi Germany.

We are, of course, forced to observe that tradition is neither unanimous nor infallible. Nor have we any right to expect it to be so. The church is not insulated from the currents of thought that flow past it and round it, and this is as it should be, since the Holy Spirit is free to impart his truth through any agents whom he may choose – even Marx and Freud. Within the church men and women of different cultures, ages and circumstances perceive and express truth in different ways; and even if what they express turns out to be different from, or even opposed to, received doctrine, that is not in itself a reason for dismissing it as false. At all points we have to take account of the obstinacy and unwillingness to change, together with the ingrained immobility of institutional religion, which runs through Christian history and has preserved doctrines for centuries which we have now learned to reject (surely 'traditional' teachings about sexuality, women and slavery are clear examples of this – and there may be more to be revealed). Above all, the Holy Spirit has seen fit from time to time to reveal 'new' truths – which are not, strictly, new, but which the church up to that time has been unable or unwilling to accept. The Orthodox theologian Vladimir Lossky has called Tradition 'the critical judgment of the church . . . made acute by the Holy Spirit'.[28]

So the body of tradition is bound to contain inconsistencies and contradictions. Attempts have been made to avoid this by limiting 'authentic' tradition to one or two channels, episcopal, presbyteral or papal. But this device, though it may temporarily produce a compact body of doctrine which the faithful may be expected to receive without reservation, does not really work. Cracks soon begin to appear, and eventually wide gaps are opened. The long-held doctrine of predestination has to be modified, women aspire to the priesthood on theological grounds and enter it, the Tridentine doctrine of transubstantiation has to be skilfully revised.

In the past, when the accredited upholders of a certain form of tradition have believed and declared their version to be the one and only possible Christian one, they have tended to become proud and intolerant. Those dubbed heretical and subversive have responded, sometimes by passive resistance, sometimes by an equal pride and arrogance. The disastrous and blasphemous wars of religion, and the harsh persecutions, have been the result. In the ecumenical age we have found a better way of dealing with our different versions of the tradition, though not all Christian bodies have adopted it. The 'better way' is consultation and reconciliation, sometimes leading to the discovery that our differences are verbal, not substantial, or cultural not theological. Some differences, of course, will still remain, but some of them are shown to be invaluable within the rich variety of the church's life, nw that they are no longer the foci of partisanship, hostility or contempt.

The denominational and other variations of the tradition can, in fact, be divided into two classes. (*a*) Those which in the course of the ecumenical conversation have been already reconciled or are on the way to being reconciled. Such are the different doctrines of justification, of the nature of the church, of the meaning of the eucharist; and many areas of the doctrine of the ministry. (*b*) Those which so far have been deemed intractable, such as the Roman Catholic doctrine of the Pope's infallibility, the Roman Catholic-Orthodox-Anglican insistence on the historic episcopacy, and the English-Anglican system of the appointment of bishops by the State. The Baptist doctrine of Believers' Baptism, and the Roman Catholic-Orthodox-Anglo-Catholic-Evangelical (not Anglican)subordination of women, leading to refusal to ordain them to the priesthood in some Anglican churches, and the opposite view held in most non-episcopal churches and most of Anglicanism, can be said to hover at present between the two classes.

But how to distinguish between true and false? The basic requirement in the ecumenical dialogue is that all concerned should be willing to submit their version or versions of Christian truth to the criterion which is also to be applied to the scriptural part of tradition: do they truly declare, clarify, expound or explicate the gospel revealed in the New Testament, or not? If the answer is Yes, they have made good their claim to a place in tradition. There is, of course, at present available no 'Supreme Court' to adjudge such claims; the best that can be done is to ask the World Council of Churches to begin to act in concert with the Roman Catholic Church towards the summoning of an Ecumenical Council. Meanwhile the World Council, the Roman Catholic Church and the individual communions must form their own judgments in relative isolation from each other and sometimes in partial collaboration; even this provisional arrangement has sometimes created an unexpected consensus. The attainment of the objective lies in the completion and fulfilment of the ecumenical process.

A Methodist reading this must ask (and members of other denominations, perhaps, likewise) whether such a view of tradition is compatible with the tradition as it has been passed down in his church and with its own traditions. But the question need not prove a difficult one for Methodists (I cannot speak for others). There is no conflict in the present proposal with the Methodist convictions that the revelation contained in scriptures provides the 'supreme rule of faith and practice', and that the teachings of John Wesley, and their development since his death, are (alongside the tested teachings of other churches) authentic parts of the tradition by which the Spirit has guided, and is still guiding, the People of God into all the truth, as the truth is in Jesus.

A REFORMED VIEW

David M. Thompson

Tradition is not a subject which has figured largely in theological reflection among the Free Churches. In some ways this is not surprising, since the affirmation that scripture is the only test of that which is necessary for salvation is a common Protestant principle. Article 6 of the Thirty-Nine Articles of the Church of England summarizes the *sola scriptura* principle of the Reformation:

> Holy Scripture containeth all things necessary to salvation: so that whatsoever is not read therein, nor may be proved thereby, is not to be required of any man, that it should be believed as an article of the Faith, or be thought requisite or necessary to salvation.

More interesting perhaps is the fact that in an age when biblical criticism has come to be taken for granted, Free Church theologians have not usually seen any point in turning their attention to tradition as a tool for determining normative interpretations of scripture. In part this exposes the unhealthy gap which currently exists between academic critical theology and week-by-week preaching and teaching in local congregations. But it also draws attention to the largely unselfconscious way in which most people take for granted the normative nature of their own tradition – in this case a Free Church tradition – without recognizing that this was largely what the Reformers were attacking. This essay is particularly concerned with the approach to tradition in the Reformed churches in England, especially as represented today by the United Reformed Church, which includes former Congregationalists, Presbyterians and Churches of Christ (Disciples); but some of the points raised are true of the Free Church tradition as a whole.

'The Bible and the Bible only is the religion of Protestants.' William Chillingworth's oft-quoted words, tinged slightly by the irony that he was the godson of Archbishop Laud and a firm supporter of Charles I, have helped to form a picture of Reformed attitudes to the relation between scripture and tradition that continues to influence instinctive responses even though much has changed since 1638. The origin of this picture goes back to John Calvin himself, who began his Geneva Confession of Faith of 1536 with these words:

> First we affirm that we desire to follow Scripture alone as rule of faith and religion, without mixing with it any other thing which might be devised by the opinion of men apart from the Word of God, and without wishing to accept for our spiritual government any other doctrine than what is conveyed to us by the same Word without addition or diminution, according to the command of our Lord.[1]

Seventeenth-century Reformed confessions of faith also commonly began with an affirmation of the authority of scripture. The Westminster Confession of 1646, which was largely drafted by Englishmen though it became normative for Presbyterianism when adopted by the General Assembly of the Church of Scotland in 1647, followed the pattern set by the Second Helvetic Confession of 1566 in entitling its first article, 'Of Holy Scripture'. Paragraph 6 stated that

> The whole counsel of God, concerning all things necessary

for his own glory, man's salvation, faith, and life, is either expressly set down in Scripture, or by good and necessary consequence may be deduced from Scripture; unto which nothing at any time is to be added, whether by new revelations of the Spirit, or traditions of men.[2]

Paragraph 9 went on to state that 'the infallible rule of interpretations of Scripture is the Scripture itself', while paragraph 10 made the 'Holy Spirit speaking in the Scripture' the supreme judge for determining all religious controversies, decrees of councils and opinions of ancient and more recent writers. This first chapter remained unaltered in the Savoy Declaration of 1658, which became the basis for English Congregationalism.

The emphasis on scripture here represents the high common ground of British (and continental) protestantism, rather than an extreme position. But the full text makes it very clear how far this position is from later theories of verbal inspiration. Certainly paragraph 8 regarded the Hebrew text of the Old Testament and the Greek text of the New as 'immediately inspired by God, and by his singular care and providence kept pure in all ages'; but paragraph 6, as well as affirming the appropriateness of making deductions from scripture, also acknowledged 'the inward illumination of the Spirit of God to be necessary for the saving understanding of such things as are revealed in the Word' and that certain matters concerning worship and church government were 'to be ordered by light of nature and Christian prudence'. Thus *The Form of Presbyterial Church Government* and *The Institution of Churches and the Order Approved in them by Jesus Christ* were separate documents from the Westminster Confession and the Savoy Declaration respectively. Both cited scripture to support the particular form of church government they commend, whether presbyterian or congregational, but the main point of each was to establish the distinctness of church government from that of the state.

This is an important clue to the Reformers' antagonism to human opinion, which is discussed more fully in chapter 10 of Book 4 of Calvin's *Institutes*. The title of this chapter is 'Of the Power of Making Laws', and it is mainly concerned with the oppressive nature of the rules imposed on people by the Pope. It is a significant reminder of the extent to which the Reformation controversies were formulated in legal terms, reflecting the way in which mediaeval ecclesiology was dominated by the structure of canon law. Calvin himself studied law at Orléans before returning to Paris to study theology, and the *Institutes* provide an orderly framework for the Reformed religion. The issue, as Calvin poses it, is 'whether the church may lawfully bind consciences by its laws'.[3] He continues,

> It has become common usage to call all decrees concerning the worship of God put forward by men apart from his Word 'human traditions'. Our contention is against these, not against holy and useful church institutions which provide for the preservation of discipline or honesty or peace.[4]

The distinction is important. Christ's condemnation of the Pharisees in Matthew 15.6 – 'So, for the sake of your tradition, you have made void the word of God' (RSV) – is cited, along with Paul's criticisms of false apostles, as the basis for a criticism of papal directives on fasting on Fridays, priestly celibacy, pilgrimages, veneration of saints etc. Isaiah 29.13, as quoted in Matthew 15.8–9, thus became a classic condemnation of tradition:

> This people honours me with their lips,
> but their heart is far from me;
> in vain do they worship me,
> teaching as doctrines the precepts of men (RSV).

Paul's argument in Colossians 2.23 that 'human traditions . . . deceive under the appearance of wisdom' is developed by Calvin to make the point that the deceptive character of human traditions lies precisely in the fact that 'human wit recognizes there what is its own, and embraces it, once recognized, more willingly than something truly excellent but less in accord with its vanity'.[5]

The Council of Trent's decree on the sacred books and apostolic traditions of 8 April 1546 was a defence of the teaching authority of the church. In it the Council stated that the whole truth of salvation and the rule of conduct

> are contained in written books and in unwritten traditions which were received by the apostles from the mouth of Christ himself, or else have come down to us, handed on as it were from the apostles themselves at the inspiration of the Holy Spirit.[6]

However, although the Council took care to link *libris scriptis* and *sine scripto traditionibus* by *et*, rather than using *partim . . . partim* ('partly in written books and partly in unwritten traditions'), the decree, as interpreted by theologians such as Bellarmine, became the origin of a theory that scripture and tradition were two independent sources of revelation, and therefore drove a significant wedge between Roman Catholic and Protestant understandings.[7]

On the Protestant side from the mid-seventeenth century, in what has been called the period of Reformed scholasticism, there was an intensifying tendency to regard anything that could not be directly proved from scripture as at best unnecessary and at worst wrong. In due course this commitment to the *sola scriptura* principle came to be used as a tool for the criticism of some of the Reformation confessions themselves. In the evangelical revival in late eighteenth-century Ireland, Thomas

Campbell, a Seceder Presbyterian minister who subsequently emigrated to the USA, sought to promote unity among the various branches of presbyterianism on the basis of the sufficiency of scripture. In the thirteen propositions of his *Declaration and Address* of 1809 he affirmed that 'nothing ought to be inculcated upon Christians as articles of faith, nor required of them as terms of communion, but what is expressly taught and enjoined upon them in the word of God'; that human authority has no power to impose new commands on the church, not ordained by Christ and so 'nothing ought to be received into the faith or worship of the church, or be made a term of communion amongst Christians, that is not as old as the New Testament'. Furthermore, although he allowed that 'inferences and deductions from scripture premises, when fairly inferred, may be truly called the doctrine of God's holy word', they did not bind the conscience any further than Christians perceived the connexion, and thus could never be made terms of communion. Similarly theological systems, since 'these must be in a great measure the effect of human reasoning' and must contain many inferential truths, should not be made terms of communion either. All that was necessary to belong to the church was 'a due measure of scriptural self-knowledge respecting their lost and perishing condition by nature and practice, and of the way of salvation through Jesus Christ', together with a profession of faith in and obedience to him.[8] This approach became the basis for the movement, known in the USA as Disciples and in this country as Churches of Christ, which developed in the nineteenth century. One of the most striking continuities with Calvin's *Institutes* is the emphasis on ordinances: Christian faith is still seen largely in terms of commands by God which have to be obeyed.

Campbell's position was one of the last 'pre-historical' approaches to theology, with its implicit view that any change from the New Testament was likely to be for the worse. In the nineteenth century a new awareness and appreciation of history led to more positive evaluations of change and development. The Bible itself ceased to be regarded as a seamless robe and was subjected to historical criticism. Congregationalists had abandoned subscription to human formularies as a term of communion by the time the Congregational Union adopted its Declaration of Faith, Church Order and Discipline in 1833; later in the century Presbyterian churches reworded the terms in which ministers were required to subscribe to the Westminster Confession.[9] Churches of Christ were destined to have considerable difficulty over whether a concern for Christian unity should take priority over an approach to scripture which could seem like fundamentalism (though without the pre-millennial doctrinal system usually attached to that term).

The change which had taken place by the twentieth century is well illustrated in the Presbyterian Church of England's Statement of Faith in 1956. In 1945 the General Assembly of the Church accepted the conclusion of a special committee that the Westminster Confession had lost its effectiveness as an expression of the Gospel to the contemporary world. It therefore authorized the preparation of a new statement of the Christian faith which would make it clear in what sense the Church now interpreted scripture. In the statement approved in 1956 a separate paragraph on tradition followed the paragraph affirming and defining the unique authority of Scripture:

> Christian tradition embodies the insight and experience of former generations of Christians, and the accumulated knowledge of God's dealings with His people in all ages. It is expressed in various ways: in creeds and confessions, in liturgies and hymns, in theological and devotional writings. It is transmitted through the life and worship of the Church. It is to be received humbly and thankfully yet with

discrimination, and tested always by the mind of Christ disclosed in Scripture.[10]

The next paragraph affirmed that since God's action was not confined to the past, new tasks were constantly unfolding and new truths were being discovered: by engaging with these tasks and appropriating these truths 'within the living tradition of the church, and in the light of the biblical revelation of God's nature and purpose', it was possible to enter more deeply into the knowledge of God. Thus the church had to avoid both shutting its eyes to new knowledge and succumbing to passing fashions of thought. Here was an entirely new emphasis on non-scriptural sources of knowledge and a different nuance in the understanding of scripture itself.

The Presbyterian statement reflects the way in which the ecumenical movement of the twentieth century had brought tradition back on to the theological agenda. In the Reports of the Faith and Order Conferences of 1927 in Lausanne and 1937 in Edinburgh there were references to the significance of tradition as understood by the Orthodox Churches. At Lund in 1952 there was no specific reference to tradition, but an interesting passage in the final section, 'Where do we stand?', spoke of the way in which the church has to proclaim the truth of God's revelation 'in ever-new terms, but the language and thought forms coined in history must be constantly corrected by the content of the Gospel'.[11] Between Lund and the Montreal Conference in 1964 there was a major study of tradition by the Faith and Order Commission. The result was the statement on 'Scripture, Tradition and Traditions' approved at Montreal, which is the fullest ecumenical statement on the subject to date.

The Commission's starting point was

that we are all living in a tradition which goes back to our Lord and has its roots in the Old Testament, and are all indebted to that tradition inasmuch as we have received the revealed truth, the Gospel, through its being transmitted from one generation to another. Thus we can say that we exist as Christians by the Tradition of the Gospel (the *paradosis* of the *kerygma*) testified in Scripture, transmitted in and by the Church through the power of the Holy Spirit. Tradition taken in this sense is actualized in the preaching of the Word, in the administration of the Sacraments and worship, in Christian teaching and theology, and in mission and witness to Christ by the lives of the members of the Church.[12]

Thus what is transmitted in the process of tradition is the Christian faith, 'not only as a sum of tenets, but as a living reality transmitted by the Holy Spirit'. Moreover from the beginning the question of what is the authentic Christian faith has had to be answered. The first response was that it lay in the apostolic writings, that which had been received from the apostles. But the writings had to be interpreted, so the existence of scripture as the written form of the tradition did not solve the problem of criterion: a hermeneutical principle was required.

The report did not articulate such a hermeneutical principle: but it noted, with some optimism, that modern biblical scholarship had done much to bring the churches together; and the section ended with three questions which provide, as it were, a programme for further development:

Should not the very fact that God has blessed the Church with the Scriptures demand that we emphasize more than in the past a common study of Scripture whenever representatives of the various churches meet? Should we not study more the Fathers of all periods of the Church and their interpretations of the Scriptures in the light of our ecumenical task? Does not the ecumenical situation demand that we search for the Tradition by re-examining sincerely our own particular traditions?[13]

The reports of the North American and European sections which lay behind the Montreal statement provide a valuable background to the way in which thinking about tradition has developed in the present century. The report of the European section by Professor K. E. Skydsgaard explained how the topic had become a new one for Roman Catholics as a result of the work of Möhler and Newman in the nineteenth century and Holstein, Congar and Rahner in the twentieth. Protestants had also been brought to look upon the subject differently because of biblical research and systematic considerations. Essentially what had made the difference was a new awareness of history and the historically conditioned nature of all human experience. Thus 'the appeal to Scripture, perhaps under the catchword *sola scriptura*, does not overcome the dilemma, because the ways in which we interpret the Bible are bound to "the tradition in which we have received the Scripture as our authority" '.[14] The snare of historical relativity was avoided because the Christ event as a moment in history transcends history and provides a point for the criticism of history. The words and deeds of Jesus, his life and death, and the risen Lord in their different ways break with any human tradition. The way in which human tradition continues to be criticized is through the work of the Holy Spirit. Professor Skydsgaard quoted a paper by the Congregational scholar, Daniel Jenkins, on 'Tradition and the Holy Spirit' in which he suggested that the church's action in relation to tradition had to express its recognition of the Spirit's lordship and freedom: without that the church would fall victim to the characteristic sin of traditionalism. 'No church,' he said, 'can be so completely confident of its own ability to interpret and obey the Spirit that it can assert without qualifications that its own particular historical tradition is entirely free from the same weaknesses and that it has nothing to learn from the others.'[15]

That tentativeness about any claim to infallibility is reflected in the Congregational Declaration of Faith of 1967. This was the result of some ten years' work on producing a statement which would meet new causes for scepticism and unbelief with new forms of Christian thought. Like the Presbyterian Statement it included a paragraph about tradition after its affirmation of the significance of the Bible. The word 'tradition' is nowhere used in the paragraph, except as a heading, and so the all-embracing nature of what is involved stands out more clearly:

> God requires the Church to remember its own history. He calls it to study expressions by the Church of its faith and thinking, the institutions of the Church and its standards of action, decisions by Councils, and the practice of piety; and events which display the Church's course in this world.

No period of the church's history is regarded as having an overriding claim on the church's attention, though the Apostles' and Nicene Creeds, the Te Deum and the Reformation Confessions and Catechisms are acknowledged with particular thankfulness as directing the church to the Bible's whole message. A fellowship with earlier generations is claimed in seeking to understand the questions they faced, which becomes the means through which God helps the church to answer old questions in new ways and new questions altogether.[16]

The Basis of Union of the United Reformed Church as adopted in 1972 drew on both the Presbyterian and Congregational statements for significant parts of its phraseology. There is no statement on tradition as such. However, the order of sentences in paragraph 12 is interesting in beginning with an affirmation of trinitarian faith, continuing with a statement about the life of faith, and ending with a statement about the Word of God in scripture, discerned under the guidance of the Holy Spirit:

> The United Reformed Church confesses the faith of the Church Catholic in one God, Father, Son and Holy Spirit. It acknowledges that the life of faith to which it is called is a gift of the Holy Spirit continually received in Word and Sacrament and in the common life of God's people. It acknowledges the Word of God in the Old and New Testaments, discerned under the guidance of the Holy Spirit, as the supreme authority for the faith and conduct of all God's people.[17]

Later there is a confession of faith at the date of formation of the new church, followed by an affirmation of the right to make new declarations of faith as occasion may require and an acceptance of 'the witness borne to the Catholic faith by the Apostles' and Nicene Creeds', together with a recognition of the formulations and declarations of faith which have been valued by its constituent members as its own particular heritage.

These twentieth-century statements concerning tradition, therefore, not only address an issue which the seventeenth-century confessions did not face, but they also change the nature of the issue. In effect, the Presbyterian and Congregational statements are concerned with the way in which the church reflects on its historical experience. They are able to do so because historical experience is now viewed positively, rather than negatively. At least the possibility, if not the fact, of progress is conceded. But alongside this goes an equivalent admission of the possibility of error. This is not, of course, due to God, but to human failure to perceive and interpret correctly God's revelation of himself. The movement away from an understanding of revelation in propositional terms towards locating it in the life of ancient Israel, and more particularly in the life, death and resurrection of Jesus Christ, creates a greater distance between revelation and the expression or interpretation of it, even in scripture itself. Indeed one of the reasons for the kind of approach described is the absorption of scripture into tradition, rather than of tradition into scripture. Thus the issue which so concerned Calvin – what counts as authoritative commands of God – has been virtually sidestepped by a reluctance to regard anything in scripture as unaffected by the process of human transmission.

What, then, is the teaching authority of the church? Here the issues are quite fluid, and much depends on the direction one chooses to look. Within academic theology, which since Vatican II now generally includes Roman Catholics, the church does not loom large as an object of investigation, except historically. University theologians are concerned to explore a theological consensus which transcends divisions between particular churches. But theology pursued within a single church tradition is less prominent today, particularly among the Free Churches. Here at best a particular ecclesiastical tradition would be taught as one among a number; at worst it would be a series of historical footnotes to a more general understanding of the church.

England, however, is unusual in the extent to which theology can be a university discipline, separated from the churches. In Europe and North America, for different historical reasons, theological faculties are more likely to have a church affiliation, even if this is not decisively reflected in either the composition or work of the faculty concerned. Ecumenical theology, although largely carried on by the same people, has a rather different agenda. Through bilateral dialogues and the multilateral work of the World Council of Churches' Faith and Order Commission, a different kind of theological consensus, in which the church does figure, is emerging.

An important new dimension in this discussion is Roman Catholic involvement. The Roman Catholic position on tradition was modified by the Second Vatican Council in its constitution on Divine Revelation, though in some ways this is more apparent by what is not there than by what is. The original form of this constitution when proposed to the Council in the first session in 1963 was withdrawn by Pope John XXIII after a vote which revealed the strength of feeling against its presentation of a two-sourse theory of revelation – scripture and tradition – following the interpretation of Trent which became popular in the post-Tridentine period. The revised version no longer spoke of two independent sources, but rather of a single source, Jesus Christ, who entrusted his gospel to his apostles. The apostles passed on what they had received, and 'some apostles, with others of the apostolic age, committed the message of salvation to writing'. The apostles entrusted their teaching function to their successors, the bishops:

> By this link, this sacred tradition and the sacred scripture of the two testaments are like a mirror in which the church, during its pilgrimage on earth, contemplates God, the source of all that it has received, until it is brought to see him face to face as he is (see I John 3.2).[18]

The succession of teachers ensures that the church can hand on what it is and believes to the next generation: the Holy Spirit assists the growth in understanding which takes place, and the fathers of the church bear witness to this work of the Spirit. Bishop Christopher Butler, who had been active in the Council's discussion of the matter, commented that this section was 'practically a précis of Newman's theory of the development of doctrine'; and he also noted the significance of the Council's use of the singular 'tradition' rather than Trent's plural 'traditions'.[19]

The constitution concludes that sacred tradition and scripture are thus bound together in a close and reciprocal relationship;

and (in a phrase which was the result of last-minute amendments in the final session of the Council) 'the church's certainty about all that is revealed is not drawn from holy scripture alone; both scripture and tradition are to be accepted and honoured with like devotion and reverence.' Moreover the authentic interpretation of the word of God, whether in scripture or tradition, is entrusted only to those charged with the teaching function of the church, though this is not above the word of God but at its service.

> Thus it is clear that, by God's wise design, tradition, scripture and the church's teaching function are so connected and associated that one does not stand without the others, but all together, and each in its own way, subject to the action of the one holy Spirit, contribute effectively to the salvation of souls.[20]

The significance of the move away from a two-source theory is clear from this summary; but it is equally clear that *Dei Verbum*, whilst including much of the emphasis on the continual activity of the Holy Spirit in the life of the church which has appealed to Protestant scholars, also affirms strongly an established teaching authority in the church in the episcopate. It is therefore vital that the continuing discussion of tradition does not get trapped in the rather arid desert that ecumenical discussions of the ministry have tended to become.

The rediscovery of the significance of tradition is due to a new sense of the dynamic process by which truth is passed from one generation to another. Seen from a human perspective it is difficult to argue that any one age or person has the authority to declare a normative truth, except in so far as this can be demonstrated by agreed processes of verification. Thus the Enlightenment in opening up the scope of human history also brought with it an almost inescapable relativism. From a

Christian perspective, however, faith that the Holy Spirit is at work in history and can be discerned by the faithful opens up another possibility, in which the community of the faithful can declare God's saving purpose to humanity in new ways appropriate to the contemporary situation. Here scripture, as the apostolic record of the proclamation of the Gospel, performs a critical function in testing every new proclamation. The great insight of the Reformers was to perceive this necessary critical role of scripture; where they fell short was in supposing that a critical principle could be substituted for the continuous process of handing on the Gospel. In fact they never did so completely: they prepared confessions of faith, and Calvin's catechism was based upon the Apostles' Creed. But there was a tendency on their part to freeze scripture into a body of propositional truths, much as the disciples of Thomas Aquinas had done before them; and this was not particularly surprising since their mental outlooks were shaped by the same scholastic process of medi- aeval theology.

Any escape from this impasse can only be an ecumenical one. No tradition by itself has the breadth of resources to enable it to progress on its own. The bilateral dialogues with the Roman Catholic Church are particularly interesting in offering ways forward.

The Roman Catholic-Reformed international dialogue, whose final report, *The Presence of Christ in Church and World*, was published in 1977, after recording agreement on some of the norms for the church found in the New Testament, acknow- ledges that the church assumes different forms according to its historical heritage and the social and cultural situation in which it is set. Whilst it is recognized that theology had to seek the normative within the relativity of historical circumstances, the report does not elucidate any normative criteria. The discussion of tradition comes in the section on the teaching authority of the church. The report acknowledges that the historical alternatives of 'scripture and tradition' and 'scripture only', as presented in the post-Tridentine period, are no longer an appropriate way of defining the problem. The New Testament writings are now seen as themselves the outcome of and witness to tradition, and the canonization of the New Testament is regarded as part of the development of tradition. Thus it is impossible to regard scripture and tradition as two different sources. So the Commission is able to say:

> We are agreed that as *creatura Verbi* the Church together with its Tradition stands under the living Word of God and that the preacher and teacher of the Word is to be viewed as servant of the Word (cf. Luke 1.2) and must teach only what the Holy Spirit permits him to hear in the Scriptures . . . We are agreed that the development of doctrine and the production of confessions of faith is a dynamic process. In this process the Word of God proves its own creative, critical and judging power. Through the Word, therefore, the Holy Spirit guides the Church to reflection, conversion and reform.[21]

Moreover because God's Word is heard in different ways in different traditions, because scripture is written in the language and concepts of the ancient world, and because we are more aware of the internal diversity of scripture today, 'the church is compelled and obliged constantly to reinterpret the biblical message'.

Interestingly, a similar concern for hermeneutics emerges in the Reformed-Baptist international dialogue report:

> We have noticed again and again that biblical interpretation is more than just finding out 'what the Bible says' and that we have to take into account various factors on the part of the interpreters . . . There was also agreement on the

necessity to discriminate between what is read into the Scripture and what is objectively given in it.[22]

On the last point, however, there was some difference of emphasis within each of the two traditions, with some wanting to find mutual correction in interpretation by close contact with Christians of other traditions and others clinging to the normative significance of scripture despite the difficulties.

The Reformed-Roman Catholic report agrees that 'the Church has its authority to the extent that it listens to the Word Christ speaks to it ever afresh',[23] but it is clear that Roman Catholic thought has room for a concept of the development of doctrine, possibly because of a difference in pneumatology: 'Catholic thought is primarily sustained by confidence in the *continuing* presence of the Spirit as a *constantly renewed* gift of the ascended Lord'.[24] Disappointingly there is no comment on the Reformed understanding of pneumatology in this context; instead the emphasis is placed on the Word of God constantly creating understanding of itself afresh in the life of the church, on the basis of a theologically trained ministry and a theologically informed congregation.[25]

Both agree that scripture derives its normative significance from the fact that it represents the apostolic witness; but they recognize that it is a continuing task 'to explicate and to ensure respect for the not merely historical but also theological precedence of the apostolic period'. Thus while the task of reformulating its faith is a continuous one for the church, there is an underlying continuity of meaning. One important difference, however, lies in the fact that for Roman Catholics the pastoral ministry has a distinct responsibility which is not derived from the believing community, whereas for Reformed the community as a whole is responsible and delegates qualified people for this task. Hence Roman Catholics are able to assert that God's faithfulness to his church means that those specially charged with the teaching mission cannot fall into error, whilst the Reformed regard God's fidelity to his covenant as alone properly infallible, and through this covenant he corrects and preserves his church by the Spirit until the consummation of his reign.[26] Whilst the report registers some important agreements, there is clearly more work to be done here.

Another hopeful way forward is emerging in the work of the Disciples-Roman Catholic International Commission. Here significant progress has been made using the biblical concept of memory. In 1987 the Commission began to explore the difference it makes to see the preservation of memory as the primary means of securing apostolic continuity, understood as the work of the Holy Spirit:

> It is the Spirit who links the past with the present, and maintains the memory of that on which everything depends – the faith itself and the church which embodies that faith. Through the Spirit therefore the power of what is remembered is made present afresh, and succeeding generations appropriate the event remembered . . . To remain in the memory of the apostolic faith the Church always needs to be recalled to an authentic and faithful witness. Teaching which is authentic is that which builds up the unity and communion of the Church, across space and time, in the truth. From the earliest times also the prophetic role has been linked to the apostolic, since the Spirit reminds us of what may have been forgotten.[27]

This inevitably directed attention to the work of the ministry.[28] However, even in a tradition which had made so much of the principle of New Testament Christianity as the Disciples, this was a natural movement. Alexander Campbell, Thomas Campbell's son, wrote in an early essay that it was 'not the will of Jesus Christ . . . that the church should be governed by a *written* document alone'. Hence wherever the apostles gathered a community together, they appointed elders (overseers or bishops) to preach, teach, and preside over the affairs of the community.[29]

The characteristic Churches of Christ thinking about the ministry (reflecting the presbyterian roots from which it sprang) may be expressed in three fundamental principles: that all are God's people; that the ministry is not *over* the church, but *of* the church; and that there is definite authority of *office* which is conferred by Christ in his church, though it is authority involving *service*.[30] The chief responsibilities of the ministry are the preaching of the gospel and the presidency at the sacraments. Preaching is more than teaching or telling a story. The *kerygma* is

> the preaching or announcing of the objective fact of the incarnate, crucified and risen Christ, so that these events *become events once more in the faith of the hearer* who receives the Gospel. The Apostles were stewards, speaking in Christ's stead, witnessing to these events; and when they did this, the amazing thing happened that the crucified and risen Christ again encountered men and women.[31]

Similarly another early Disciple writer, Walter Scott, wrote that baptism and the Lord's Supper 'are the crucifixion, or death, burial, and resurrection of Christ, repeating themselves in the life and profession of the disciples, and proclaiming to the ages that he, that was to come, is come'.[32] The work of the ministry reaches a climax at the Lord's Supper where the one who presides not only re-tells the story but also re-enacts the breaking of the bread and the pouring of the wine using the dominical words. This is what *Baptism, Eucharist and Ministry* calls 'the visible focus of the deep and all-embracing communion between Christ and the members of his body'. Significantly the report continues, 'In the celebration of the eucharist, Christ gathers, teaches and nourishes the Church. It is Christ who invites to the meal and who presides at it.'[33] Because the ministry stands at this intersection of the divine-human encounter, it is very important to decide which side it is on.

The Reformed affirmation is that even here the ministry is part of the human side of the church, rather than the divine: it is the Holy Spirit which takes the thing of Christ and declares them to the church, 'so that they again become "event" in the life of the church; and it is those who abide in the word who are in true relationship to the Spirit'.[34] Moreover, the significance of the Christian view that authority lies in service is seen also in the relationship which must exist between the ministry and the church as a whole. The truth that the character of god is redemptive love cannot simply be taught; it must be lived. This is the significance of the fellowship of the church.

Thus it also seems important to those in the Reformed tradition to emphasize the priority of the church over the ministry, in the sense that the church as a whole is the body of Christ. But the idea that ministers are delegates of the church, as suggested earlier in the Reformed-Roman Catholic Dialogue report, is an unhappy choice of phrase from the Reformed point of view. Bernard Manning, a Congregational layman, once made the point sharply in an ordination address:

> At your hands indeed he receives the commission; but it is Christ's commission, not yours; and it comes from Christ, not you. When your minister speaks mark whose word it is that he speaks. You do not hear from him an echo of your own voice. It is the Word of God that he proclaims, no word that you have committed to him to-night. The minister is not the creation of the Church. The Church is sometimes his creation.[35]

The issue here is another example of the problem of relating the divine and the human, entirely analogous to the way in which we want to say that the Bible contains human words and human expressions and yet contains the Word of God. Thus the Reformed assert that Christ appoints his ministers, but that he does so through the Church.[36]

The difference between Reformed and Roman Catholic at this point once more concerns the extent to which any particular human state of affairs is to be given divine sanction. The issue is clearly put in the United Reformed Church's Response to *Baptism, Eucharist and Ministry* when it states, in relation to the ministry, that 'it is not clear why the Spirit might not have been as much at work in the breakdown of the threefold pattern in the sixteenth and seventeenth centuries as in the creation of it in the second and third'.[37] The same point emerges in the Congregational Declaration of Faith of 1967, when it declares that no age has any particular priority. There is an openness about the study to which the Church is called:

> God calls his Church to scrutinize its life hitherto with open historical attentiveness; to consider the experience of any who have claimed the Christian name whether or not they satisfy particular theological standards for being the Church; and to discern where in past times Christian communities were obedient and where they were disobedient.[38]

The reason for this openness is that God is faithful to those who are faithful to him, and even to those who are unfaithful to him. There is always the possibility that some part of the apostolic memory may have been preserved in any part of the church.

Succession and tradition always need, therefore, to be read inclusively rather than exclusively. The first nonconformists were Anglicans and the first Protestants were Roman Catholics

– something which is often forgotten. Our traditions cannot simply be understood retrospectively, since this always puts the emphasis on difference and breaking away rather than on continuity. Traditions need to be understood in terms of their origins.

It may therefore be helpful to conclude with a reference to the Old Testament, by which Reformed Christians have always been fascinated. Christianity itself has an ambiguous relationship with the Old Testament. On the one hand, it is the foundation for the understanding of Christ; on the other hand, Christianity was born out of a conflict with religious tradition. This is why Professor Skydsgaard in the report prepared for Montreal concluded that the crucial point of the ecumenical problem consisted in the relationship between Israel and the Christian church. Here lies the significance of the Faith and Order Commission's observation in that report that Jesus was a Jew; and that Paul's discussion of the dilemma of the purposes of God in Romans 9–11 is crucial to a proper understanding of our situation. The Reformed characteristically see in this the sovereignty of God's grace, not understood in some overpowering way that renders human response meaningless, but in an enabling way which guarantees that his purpose will always be fulfilled. Perhaps therefore Paul's conclusion at the end of his discussion is the only appropriate one: 'O the depth of the riches and wisdom and knowledge of God! How unsearchable are his judgments and how inscrutable his ways . . . For from him and through him and to him are all things. To him be glory for ever. Amen.'[39]

Notes

Introduction

1. Anglican-Roman Catholic International Commission, *The Final Report*, CTS/SPCK 1982, pp. 70f.

A Baptist View

1. See E. A. Payne, *The Fellowship of Believers. Baptist Thought and Practice Yesterday and Today*, Carey Kingsgate Press 1952, p. 144.
2. Payne, op. cit., p. 19.
3. Robert Robinson, quoted in H. Leon McBeth, *The Baptist Heritage*, Broadman Press 1987, p. 47f.
4. SCM Press 1944.
5. For a recent attempt at 'retrieving' the Baptist tradition of ecclesiology see the collection of essays by P. S. Fiddes, R. Hayden, R. L. Kidd, K. W. Clements and B. Haymes, *Bound to Love. The covenant basis of Baptist life and mission*, Baptist Union 1985.
6. In W. L. Lumpkin, *Baptist Confessions of Faith*, Judson Press 1969, p. 250.
7. R. P. C. Hanson, 'Tradition' in Alan Richardson and John Bowden (eds), *A New Dictionary of Christian Theology*, SCM Press 1983, pp. 574-6.
8. Lumpkin, op. cit., p. 235.
9. N. Clark, 'The Fulness of the Church of God' in A. Gilmore (ed.), *The Pattern of the Church. A Baptist View*, Lutterworth Press 1963, p. 93.
10. *Baptism, Eucharist and Ministry* (Faith and Order Paper 111), World Council of Churches 1982, p. x.
11. In M. Thurian (ed.), *Churches Respond to BEM. Official Responses to the 'Baptism, Eucharist and Ministry' Text Vol. I*, (Faith and Order Paper 129), World Council of Churches 1986, p. 73.
12. R. Gregor Smith, Chapter 1 'Faith and Doctrine', *The Doctrine of God*, Collins 1970.

13. In A. Flannery (ed.), *Vatican Council II. The Conciliar and Post-Conciliar Documents Vol. I*, Fowler Wright 1975, p. 751.
14. Ibid., p. 753.
15. Ibid., p. 754.
16. Ibid.
17. Ibid., pp. 754f.
18. Ibid., p. 756.
19. In H.-G. Link (ed.), *Apostolic Faith Today. A Handbook for Study* (Faith and Order Paper 124), World Council of Churches 1985, pp. 81.f.
20. Ibid., p. 82.
21. P. Avis, *Ecumenical Theology and the Elusiveness of Doctrine*, SPCK 1986, p. 61.
22. Rosemary Radford Ruether, *Faith and Fratricide*, Seabury Press, New York 1974.
23. R. Gregor Smith, op. cit., p. 28.
24. SCM Press 1990.
25. Ibid., p. 143.
26. Ibid., p. 88.
27. SCM Press 1987.
28. Ian Sellars, 'Edwardians, Anabaptists and the Problem of Baptist Origins', *Baptist Quarterly XXIX* (1981–82), pp. 97–112.
29. Christopher Ellis, *Together on the Way. A Theology of Ecumenism*, British Council of Churches 1990, p. 72.
30. Elisabeth Schüssler Fiorenza, *In Memory of Her. A Feminist Reconstruction of Christian Origins*, SCM Press 1983, p. 33.
31. R. Gregor Snmith, op. cit., p. 31.
32. Foreword to Payne, *Fellowship of Believers* (see n.1).

A Methodist View

1. *Preface to Sermons on Several Occasions*, Vol. I, para. 5, Bicentennial Edition of *The Works of John Wesley*, Vol. 1: *Sermons I* ed. A. C. Outler, Abingdon Press, Nashville 1984, p. 105.
2. Ibid.
3. Ibid.
4. *c*. 330–*c*. 395.
5. *c*. 347–407.
6. *c*. 337–379.
7. *c*. 342–420.

8. *c.* 354–430.
9. *c.* 300–*c.* 390. But the writings traditionally ascribed to him were perhaps written by another hand, and in Syria rather than Egypt.
10. *c.* 306–373. His works were written mainly in verse.
11. fl. *c.* 96.
12. 69–*c.* 155.
13. *c.* 35–*c.* 107.
14. 1516–1587.
15. See Bicentennial Edition of *The Works of John Wesley*, Vol. 9: *The Methodist Societies* ed. Rupert E. Davies, Abingdon Press, Nashville 1989, pp. 31, 32.
16. In his *Account of the Primitive Church* (1691). He was afterwards Lord Chancellor.
17. 1635–1699. In his *Irenicon* (1659).
18. Henry D. Rack in *Reasonable Enthusiast*, Epworth Press 1989, p. 292, holds that Wesley had reached his own conclusions about episcopacy for practical reasons, and then called on King and Stillingfleet to confirm them. This contradicts Wesley's own account of the matter in his *Journal*, III 22.
19. The development in American Methodism was quite different. See H. P. Heitzenrater, *Mirror and Memory*, Abingdon Press, Nashville 1989, pp. 189 ff.
20. See W. Strawson in *A History of the Methodist Church in Great Britain* Vol. 3 ed. Davies, George and Rupp, Epworth Press 1983, pp. 213 ff.
21. 'The Methodist Church claims and cherishes its place in the Holy Catholic Church which is the Body of Christ. It rejoices in the inheritance of the Apostolic Faith and loyally accepts the fundamental principles of the historic creeds and of the Protestant Reformation. It ever remembers that in the Providence of God Methodism was raised up to spread Scriptural Holiness through the land by the proclamation of the Evangelical Faith and declares its unfaltering resolve to be true to its Divinely appointed mission.

    The Doctrines of the Evangelical Faith which Methodism has held from the beginning and still holds are based upon the Divine revelation recorded in the Holy Scriptures. The Methodist Church acknowledges this revelation as the supreme rule of faith and practice. These Evangelical Doctrines to which the Preachers of The Methodist Church both Ministers and Laymen are pledged are contained in Wesley's Notes on the New Testament and the first four volumes of his sermons.

The Notes on the New Testament and the 44 Sermons are not intended to impose a system of formal or speculative theology on Methodist Preachers, but to set up standards of preaching and belief which should secure loyalty to the fundamental truths of the Gospel of Redemption and ensure the continued witness of the Church to the realities of the Christian experience of salvation.

Christ's Ministers in the Church are Stewards in the household of God and Shepherds of His flock. Some are called and ordained to this sole occupation and have a principal and directing part in these great duties but they hold no priesthood differing in kind from that which is common to all the Lord's people and they have no exclusive title to the preaching of the gospel or the care of souls. These ministries are shared with them by others to whom also the Spirit divides His gifts severally as He wills.

It is the universal conviction of the Methodist people that the office of the Christian Ministry depends upon the call of God who bestows the gifts of the Spirit the grace and the fruit which indicate those whom He has chosen.

Those whom The Methodist Church recognizes as called of God and therefore receives into its Ministry shall be ordained by the imposition of hands as expressive of the Church's recognition of the Minister's personal call. The Methodist Church holds the doctrine of the priesthood of all believers and consequently believes that no priesthood exists which belongs exclusively to a particular order or class of men but in the exercise of its corporate life and worship special qualifications for the discharge of special duties are required and thus the principle of representative selection is recognized.

The Preachers itinerant and lay are examined tested and approved before they are authorized to minister in holy things. For the sake of Church Order and not because of any priestly virtue inherent in the office the Ministers of The Methodist Church are set apart by ordination to the Ministry of the Word and Sacraments.

The Methodist Church recognizes two sacraments namely Baptism and the Lord's Supper as of Divine Appointment and of perpetual obligation of which it is the privilege and duty of Members of The Methodist Church to avail themselves.

22. I have attempted to carry out this process of stripping away in my *Making Sense of the Creeds*, Epworth Press 1987.

23. There was for a time considerable dispute as to which *are* the 'Forty-Four Sermons' here mentioned, as the first four volumes of the *Sermons* differed in different eighteenth-century editions. It was finally decided, with legal help, in 1914 that the Forty-Four Sermons referred to are to be found in the first four volumes of the 1787–8 edition. There is a full discussion of this matter in R. P. Heitzenrater, *Mirror and Memory*, pp. 182 f.

24. The documents are to be found in *Statements of the Methodist Church on Faith and Order, 1933–1983*, Methodist Publishing House 1984.

25. *The Fourth World Conference on Faith and Order. The Report from Montreal, 1963*, ed. P. C. Rodger and L. Vischer, SCM Press 1964, pp. 51f.

26. See n. 25 above.

27. From the *Report of the Edinburgh Faith and Order Conference, 1937*, quoted in the *Report of Conversations between the Church of England and the Methodist Church*, SPCK 1963.

28. Quoted with approval by Professor Rowan Williams in his address to a conference on 'Affirming Catholicism' in June 1990, subsequently published by Mainstream, St Mary le Bow, Cheapside, London EC2V 6AU.

A Reformed View

1. J. K. S. Reid (ed.) *Calvin: Theological Treatises*, Library of Christian Classics XXII, SCM Press 1954, p. 26.

2. David M. Thompson (ed.), *Stating the Gospel: Formulations and Declarations of Faith from the Heritage of the United Reformed Church*, T.&T. Clark 1990, pp. 13–14.

3. John T. McNeill (ed.), *Calvin: Institutes of the Christian Religion*, Library of Christian Classics XXI, SCM Press 1961, p. 1179.

4. Ibid., p. 1180.

5. Ibid., p. 1189.

6. Norman P. Tanner S. J. (ed.), *Decrees of the Ecumenical Councils*, Sheed & Ward and Georgetown University Press 1990, vol.ii, p. 663.

7. *The Old and the New in the Church* (WCC Faith and Order Paper 34), SCM Press 1961, p. 23.

8. Thompson, *Stating the Gospel*, pp. 136–7 (propositions 3, 5–8); see also David M. Thompson, 'The Irish Background to Thomas Campbell's *Declaration and Address*', *Journal of the United Reformed Church History Society* III, May 1985, pp. 215–25.

9. For the text of the Congregational Union's Declaration of Faith, Church Order and Discipline of 1833, see Albert Peel, *These Hundred Years*, London 1931, pp. 69–74, and for R. W. Dale's criticisms, see R. W. Dale, *History of English Congregationalism*, Hodder & Stoughton 1907, pp. 699–709; for the modified form of subscription adopted by the Presbyterian Church of England in 1892, see S. W. Carruthers, *Digest of the Proceedings of the Synods of the Presbyterian Church of England, 1876–1906*, London 1907, p. 24.

10. Thompson, *Stating the Gospel*, p. 186.

11. H. N. Bate (ed.), *Faith and Order: Proceedings of the World Conference, Lausanne, August 3–21 1927*, SCM Press 1927, pp. 464–7; Leonard Hodgson (ed.), *The Second World Conference on Faith and Order, held at Edinburgh, August 3–18 1937*, SCM Press 1938, pp. 229–30, 253–4; Oliver S. Tomkins (ed.), *The Third World Conference on Faith and Order, held at Lund, August 15 to 28 1952*, SCM Press 1953, pp. 61–2.

12. P. C. Rodger & L. Vischer (eds), *The Fourth World Conference on Faith and Order, Montreal 1963*, SCM Press 1964, pp. 52–3.

13. Ibid., p. 54

14. Report of the Theological Commission on Tradition and Traditions, Faith and Order Paper 40, p. 46 in Paul S. Minear, *Faith and Order Findings*, SCM Press 1963.

15. Ibid., p. 49.

16. Thompson, *Stating the Gospel*, p. 227.

17. Ibid., p. 251.

18. Tanner, *Decrees of the Ecumenical Councils*, p. 974. For an account of the discussions at the Council, see Xavier Rynne, *Letters from Vatican City*, Faber 1963, pp. 140–73; *The Third Session*, Faber 1965, pp. 35–48; *The Fourth Session*, Faber 1966, pp. 184–96, esp. pp. 187–8.

19. B. C. Butler, *The Theology of Vatican II*, Darton, Longman & Todd 1967, pp. 40–44.

20. Tanner, *Decrees of the Ecumenical Councils*, p. 975.

21. Harding Meyer & Lukas Vischer, *Growth in Agreement* (Faith and Order Paper 108), World Council of Churches 1984, p. 440.

22. Ibid., p. 135.
23. Ibid., p. 439.
24. Ibid., p. 441.
25. Several of the confessions of faith in Lukas Vischer's volume, *Reformed Witness Today*, Berne 1982, contain a fuller reference to the Holy Spirit in this context, e.g. the Church of Jesus Christ in Madagascar (p. 17), the Presbyterian Church in USA (p. 249) and the United Reformed Church in the UK (pp. 460, 467).
26. Meyer & Vischer, *Growth in Agreement*, pp. 442–4.
27. Agreed Account of the Tenth Meeting of the Disciples of Christ-Roman Catholic International Commission for Dialogue, *Midstream* XXVII, October 1988, paras. 8, 10, pp. 442–4.
28. David M. Thompson, 'Ministry and the Re-presentation of the Apostolic Tradition', *Midstream* XXIX, July 1990, pp. 212–24.
29. A. Campbell, *Christianity Restored*, Bethany, Va. 1835, p. 176.
30. Annual Conference of Churches of Christ in Great Britain and Ireland, *Report of the Commission on the Ministry*, Birmingham 1954, pp. 5–6.
31. Ibid., p. 16..
32. W. Scott, *The Messiahship*, Cincinnati, n.d., p. 284.
33. 'Ministry', para 14, 'Baptism, Eucharist and Ministry' in Meyer & Vischer, *Growth in Agreement*, pp. 485–6.
34. *Report of the Commission on the Ministry*, pp. 17–18.
35. B. L. Manning, *A Layman in the Ministry*, London 1942, p. 153.
36. See W. Robinson, *The Biblical Doctrine of the Church*, St Louis 1955, pp. 202–3.
37. M. Thurian (ed.), *Churches respond to BEM*, World Council of Churches 1986, p. 104.
38. Thompson, *Stating the Gospel*, p. 227.
39. Romans 11.33, 36 (RSV).